Drawing Nirvana

Drawing Nirvana

Art, Poetry, Love

poems and drawings by

David Sapp

Shanti Arts Publishing
Brunswick, Maine

Drawing Nirvana
Art, Poetry, Love

Published by Shanti Arts Publishing

Shanti Arts LLC | 193 Hillside Road
Brunswick, Maine 04011 | shantiarts.com

Printed in the United States of America

All drawings are by David Sapp. They are non-objective, untitled, and created with various graphite pencils and graphite crayons on 100% cotton archival paper, 250 gsm. The drawings measure 60 x 36 or 40 x 32 inches. More drawings may be viewed on Sapp's website: davidsappdrawings.viewbook.com.

ISBN: 978-1-951651-77-0 (softcover)

Library of Congress Control Number: 2021934807

for Heidi, Em, and Andrew

Contents

Foreword *9*
Preface *11*
Acknowledgments *13*

Nirvana 17
Zen Garden 19
Love and History 21
Nervous 22

Desire 24
Just Boys 26
The Hip 29
Ocean 31

Reacquainted 33
I Carry Love 34
Cogs 37
Split 38

Imperfection 40
Aria 42
Constructivism 44
Canada 46

A Monk 49
Master and Pupil 51
Young Siddhartha 53
The Artist 55

In the Snow 56
A Saffron Moon 59
A Vision 61
The Watercourse Way 63

Laughing Buddha 65
Two Buddha 66
Paradise 69
We Fool Ourselves 70

Certainly No Nirvana 73
A Keening 75
Despite Too Many 76
Hoarder 78

Intoxication 80
Nothing Left Undone 83
Seven Years 85
Blissful Obliteration 86

Love 89
Nirvana at Last 90
Practical 92
Little Boy 94

David Sapp *97*
Allen Zimmerman *97*

Foreword

For many years now David Sapp has been a poet and visual artist of my admiration. There is a particular way he makes informed reference to philosophical traditions that I admire, a characteristically light and kindly way by which he reveals how certain philosophical and religious ideals and perceptions have contributed to his response to the world and into the working out of his life. David never shoehorns doctrine or dogma into his work. He simply suggests there are ways of thought he finds fit for his purpose, making clear to us why he finds them fitting.

I refer to such poems as "Watercourse Way," where he sees his mind moving as water moves in nature and "acting accordingly, defying / pushing at artificial edges", revealing by his use of that single word "acting" his understanding that there is nothing abstract about Lao Tzu and Siddhartha. Both teachers of a "way" would agree that what they taught (and the whole body of commentary on what they meant) is useless unless their perceptions are applied to one's own life, as the speaker in this poem is acting in accordance with a way that he finds congenial, calming, bracing, productive of thought and thoughtful art.

So life is never an abstract noun for David; he lifts specific moments out of his life that exemplify the countless trivialities of all our lives. The speaker in "Zen Garden," in a kind of revolt against the dualism of mind and body, walks the land behind his garage and is present in the contours of his driveway, making his mark "across the gravel" and stopping to look and listen, his legs and ears every bit as important as his eyes and mind. There's a truth here: we are wholly parts of the material world and perpetually engaged with the external world. "Pine needles and cones / Are scattered in usual beautiful / Patterns: haphazard and perfect." Lines like these naturally, and with rapt attention to detail, remind us how lucky we are to be a material part of the external world.

Something else this poem reveals is the poet's need to celebrate certain free, unencumbered moments when he feels weightless, cleared up—"fit for work, ready to know" in the words of a Thai Buddhist monk—rare instances of the kind of happiness enjoyed by the irrepressible "happy tramps" Han Shan and Shih Te, whose Taoist stance of cosmic laughter is invoked by the last word, "hilarious," the poet calling on his sense of the comic and absurd to counteract the deleterious effects of seeming "chaos" because, as he says in a later poem, "Laughter is likely / More practical."

More often, however, the voice in David's poems suggests a more exalted yearning for some flash of comprehensive understanding, for "a tiny ecstasy a little / Trickle of nirvana" ("A Vision"). Perhaps this yearning finds its most intense and self-obliterating expression in the aesthetic experience he attempts to communicate in "Aria," where the poet is overcome when hearing during a gathering of artists the pure voice of a single singer. Suddenly "All pretense and pettiness fall away. Instantly, this moment / is beauty. I am Saint Theresa in Ecstasy, her voice piercing / me with divinity." The poet concludes that "this, at last this, must be God's love", another indication that the poet is open to every tradition that includes reference to some kind of higher, unaccountably thrilling and overpowering experience, felt viscerally. The particular experience celebrated here is real for the poet, and yet it can only be experienced; it can never adequately be communicated in words. What's a poet to do when words no longer have the capacity to communicate?

It seems to me that David's drawings, with which each poem in this collection is paired, pick up at the point at which the words, of necessity, leave off, where there is nowhere the words can go in their always worthy attempt to express the inexpressible. When the poet can no longer adequately express, the best the visual artist can do is suggest. To me, the drawings, these pulsing, mesmerizing swirls suggest rhythms underlying seeming chaos, the chaos he refers to explicitly and implicitly in some of his poems. Each pairing of poem and image becomes an invitation to attend to both the constancy of the repeated rhythms of galactic spin and the subtle shifts and changes that differentiate one drawing from another, an invitation to consider the possibility of fleeting apprehensions of timeless all-creating power (so this is the way worlds spin) while at the same time responding to the urgencies of the moment. Viewed together these pairings seem to me to stand for constancy amid change, the eternal underpinning the diurnal, the possibility of arriving finally, however briefly, at an understanding (so this is the way the world works) even as we are making our daily rounds, tracing our way through the rituals and repetitions of our individual lives.

David's work reveals a rare combination of qualities. He is an open, honest, philosophically informed and poetically gifted, thoroughly engaged and engaging artist who continually conveys the impression that he is a celebrant of life, bent on making sense of what he encounters in his own life. It is a privilege to be a member of his audience.

Allen Zimmerman
County Kerry, Ireland

Preface

When I was an earnest young man studying at the Cleveland Institute of Art, I spent a summer pouring over the art and philosophy of the Far East. I gravitated toward Lao Tzu and Zen Buddhism though I lacked a true grasp of the concepts. I found the ideas refreshing, a new way of seeing the world. The aesthetic of brush and ink calligraphy and painting in China and Japan opened new possibilities in my art. For a short time, I intended to create my own calligraphy, but in graphite. I created what I called poetry drawings, seeking to merge a visual statement with the written word. This did not work out so well. The drawings contained far too many lines, and I had far too much to say. One could not read the poems; there was not enough space on the page. The drawing and poetry parted ways for the next forty years. The drawings became the basis for increasingly non-objective pursuits, and the poems became entirely narrative. Yet, to this day they are created side by side, in parallel play, in my little Ohio studio. They are, equally, the joy in my life. The drawings cannot be adequately defined with words, as they are, unabashedly, visual. And the poems rely exclusively upon words to convey often the same image, memory, or emotion.

The drawings and poems may need a bit of context. To say the work "speaks for itself" is rather presumptive. My primary endeavor is to actualize a work of art that embodies natural, immediate, and responsive expression. My aim is not to create the sensational or the intellectually novel, but to validate the complexity of the human presence, to find a truth in my human condition at a particular moment. A drawing or poem is initiated at a point of encounter and is often a tenuous fragment or impression. I allow the lines and words to form organically, in a place somewhere between a vibrant reality and the recesses of my unconscious. I relish the elusive aspect of this emergence and honor this transience. In the final image or poem, when the work is delivered to the viewer, it is transformed into a new, autonomous existence. At its best, a drawing or poem retains the freshness and spontaneity of the original vision.

I am rather suspicious of artists' statements, including my own rhetoric. There is a sign on my wall that reads "Just Draw." The act of drawing is this simple: I walk into the studio, pick up a pencil, and make marks of graphite on a beautiful piece of paper; I work on a poem; there is a pleasant view from my window; I listen to a Chopin Mazurka while I write. Now, the drawings and poems appear again, side by side, in this book as they do each day. I am grateful.

I have not mentioned nirvana. Any attempt to draw or write about nirvana is a silly pursuit. I do not spin prayer wheels, though I find the practice fascinating; I am generally too impatient for meditation; and my noggin remains equally mindful and mindless as I age. As a young man I knew nothing of nirvana as I had too much to express, too much to accomplish, a life of objectives and desires ahead of me. Now, as an older man, I know better.

David Sapp
Berlin Heights, Ohio

Acknowledgments

Loving gratitude goes to my dear editor and wife, Heidi, and to my children, Em and Andrew, for their unwavering support of my art and writing.

I am forever happily indebted to Allen Zimmerman, my professor and mentor, who pointed out this Watercourse Way many years ago, who understands the intent of my expression, and who provided the foreword for the book.

I am grateful to Christine Cote, editor and publisher of Shanti Arts, for providing this splendid opportunity to share these poems and drawings with the world and for her dedication to supporting the arts.

I thank Stephen Tomasko, Charles T. Mayer, and Nicholas Bielby for their friendship, keen insight, and long-time appreciation of my art and writing.

Many thanks are extended to the publications in which these poems first appeared:

The Alembic, "A Keening"
Between These Shores, "Nervous"
California Quarterly, "Ocean"
Conceit, "Desire"
Down in the Dirt, "Cogs"
The Maynard, "Imperfection"
Pennine Platform, "Nirvana," "Nirvana at Last," and "Paradise"
Gold Dust, "Aria"
Icon, "A Monk"
Miller's Pond, "Reacquainted" and "Split"
Prairie Winds, "Two Buddha"
Ravensperch, "Love"
Stand, "Constructivism"
Stray Branch, "Despite Too Many"
The MacGuffin, "Master and Pupil"
Thorny Locust, "The Artist"
Tulane Review, "Young Siddhartha"
Urthona, "Zen Garden"
West Trade Review, "The Hip" and "A Saffron Moon"
Willard and Maple, "I Carry Love"

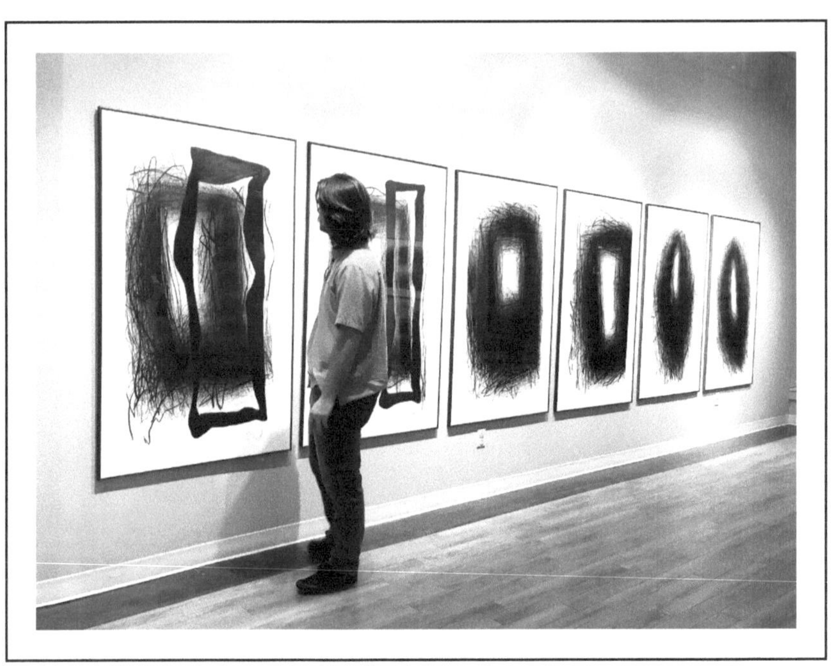

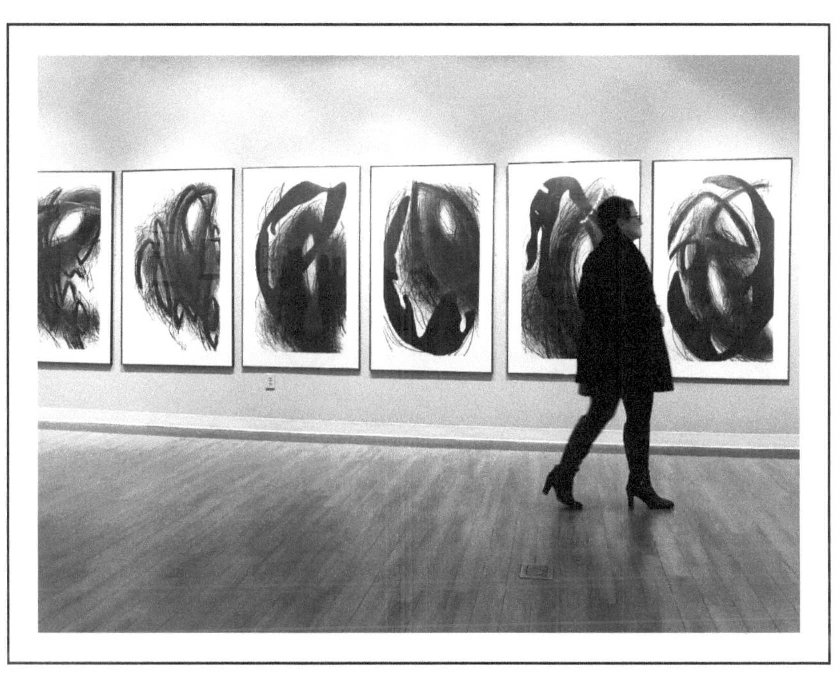

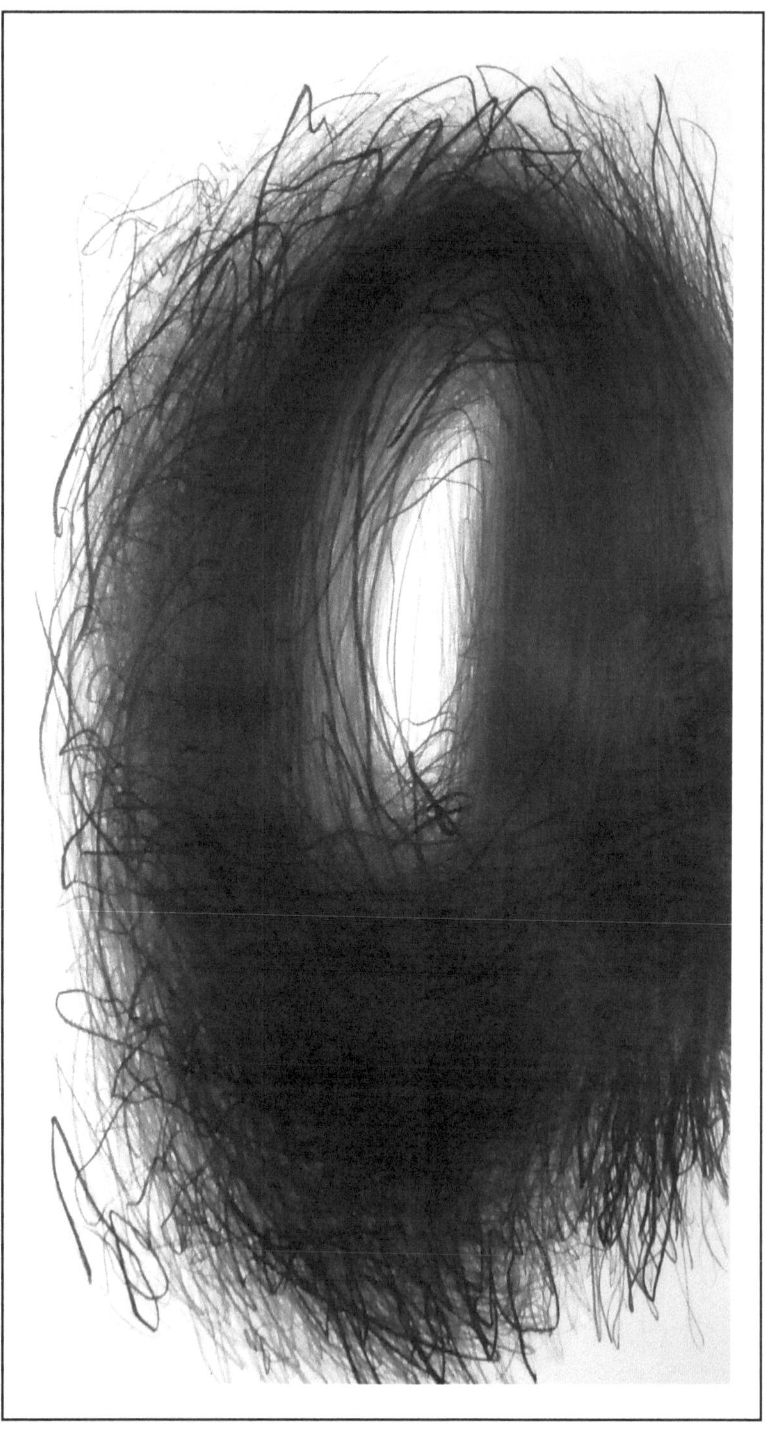

Nirvana

At Discount Drug Mart,
Between birthday and sympathy,
I pick the perfect greeting card:
"Congratulations on
Your Enlightenment."
Bon voyage! You win
An-all-expense-paid-trip
To Buddha's Bodhi Tree.
Are you giddy? That will pass.
My note inside is more
Circumspect, a little sarcastic:
Finally, nirvana! It took you
Long enough, but to be fair,
When you were young, so much
To accomplish and conquer,
Nirvana was elusive, ridiculous.
Finally, your belly bigger,
Joints stiffer, skin slack
Around the jowls, a nap
More often than meditation,
You do not contort into the lotus.
Finally awake, you're so very
Mindful, solutions are rare,
Conclusions fleeting at best,
Acutely aware of futile obsession.
Finally, your karma untangled,
Resolutions tidied, time to retire,
Suffering allayed, sins absolved,
Already contentment ho-hum,
You miss the battles, the medals.
You must admit you miss the misery.

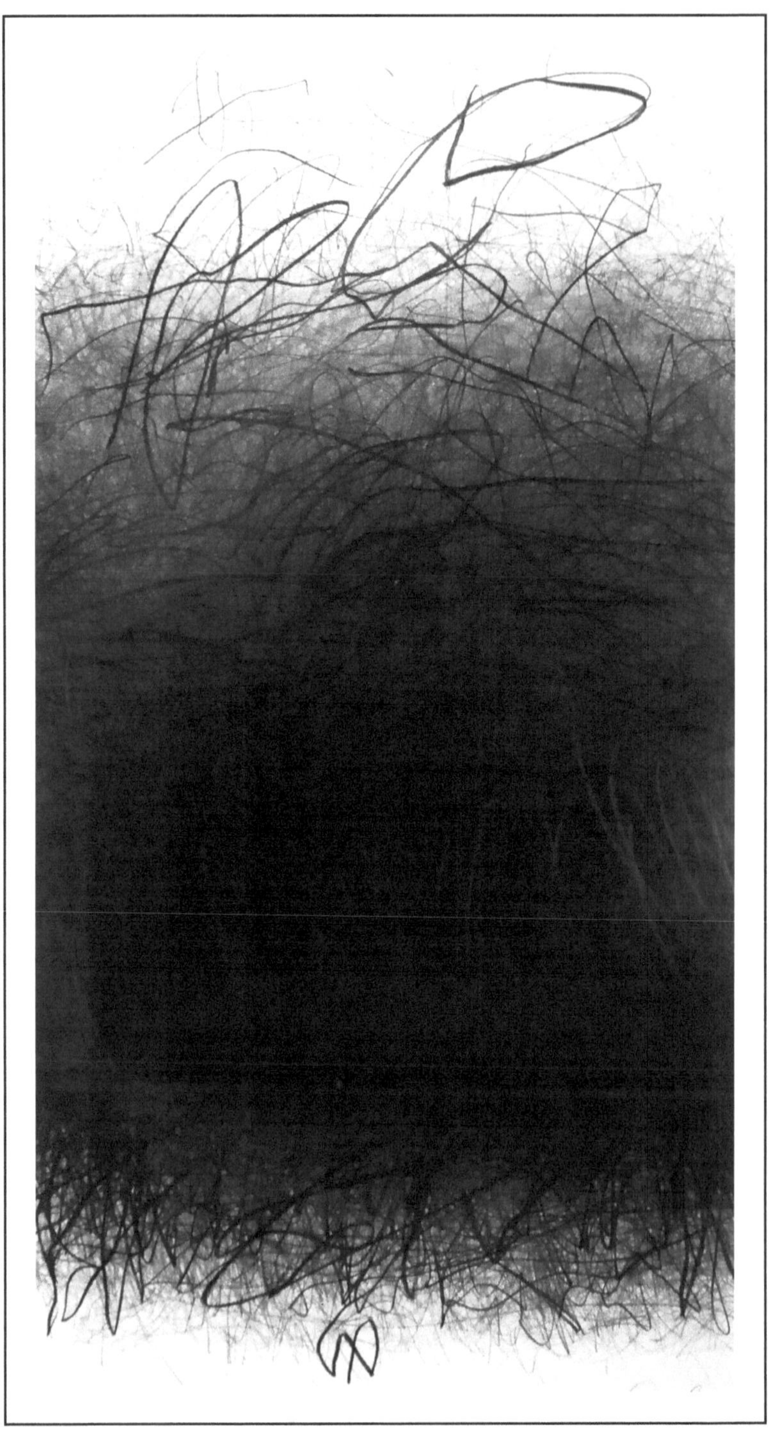

Zen Garden

Finally, I am one of those
Crazy hermits, a happy tramp,
Han-shan or Shih-te "roaring
With laughter at drifting leaves."

Out back, behind the garage,
Pine needles and cones
Are scattered in usual, beautiful
Patterns: haphazard and perfect.

But I find the rake anyway,
Not as the *bonseki* suggests
In an "unintentional intention."
No, I'm determined; I plan.

I drag across the gravel, I scribe
Harmonious lines, asymmetrical
Spaces, a Sesshu painting
Of misting mountains and rivers,
Arabesques around a lawn mower.

A few days later, the truck
Arrives to fill the tank and
The man and the fuel line
Disrupt the harmony. Perfect!

Pine needles and cones continue
To fall. Tranquility comes when
I rake again. No respite from chaos,
Finally, this is hilarious.

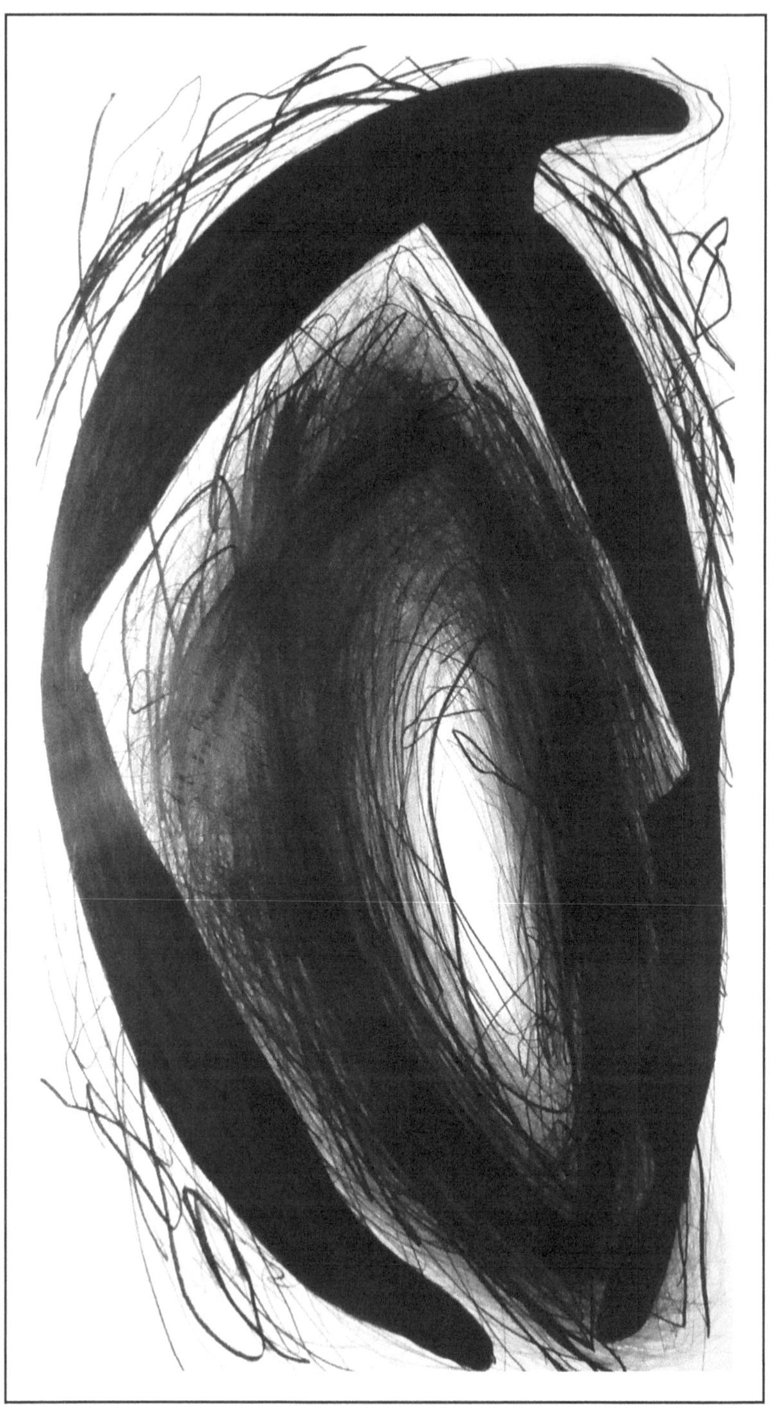

Love and History

Love and my peculiar history was hammered into steel
(Yes, by now, I am a history.) skillfully flattened
on the anvil, tempered, I suppose—inevitable, the human
narrative. But I grew brittle, weathered, rusted
on nearly every edge. Nostalgically, I recall a time,
as far as memory will allow: still sloughing my mother's
blood, the umbilicus cut but tender, first, unassuming
gasps of air suckling at new atmosphere (No one asked
if I wanted this.) before I was stolen home to play
a predictable role: the good, obedient, loving son all
rolled into one, when I was vulnerable, irresistible,
loved—loved for vulnerability, instinct insisting
upon it—cute, little roly-poly tabula rasa, all before love's
bitter tang on the tongue, the apathy, the relentless
lethargy of love. Free of love's weighty demands,
love wasn't an assumption, an accruing of love's equity.
Love did not yet own me, and I did not pursue
the expertise to enslave love for my purpose. Love did not
require a deal, intricate negotiations for affection.
This was a primordial era before love was a notion,
a religion, a dogma, an ideal. Innocence was pure
as love's expectations were hypothetical. I've spent
these last years longing for a return to that bliss.

Nervous

I was always a nervous
Little boy, negotiating
Playground perils,
The bigger, louder
Boys, girls, figuring
When and how to kiss
Patty under the wild
Cherry tree. (The why
Remained an enigma.)
My apprehension
Loomed from more
Malevolent origins:
A dark violence,
A cruel neglect,
Too many horrific events,
A long list efficiently
Repressed. (But we won't
Get into that, will we?)
My symptoms manifested:
My belly, a perpetually
Clenched little fist;
My frequent and
Spontaneous bloody
Nose on the school bus;
My peculiar and relentless
Obsessions and compulsions.
Now gray, nearly sixty,
That small, anxious child
Huddles, cringes,
Desperate for a quiet,
Unobtrusive corner.

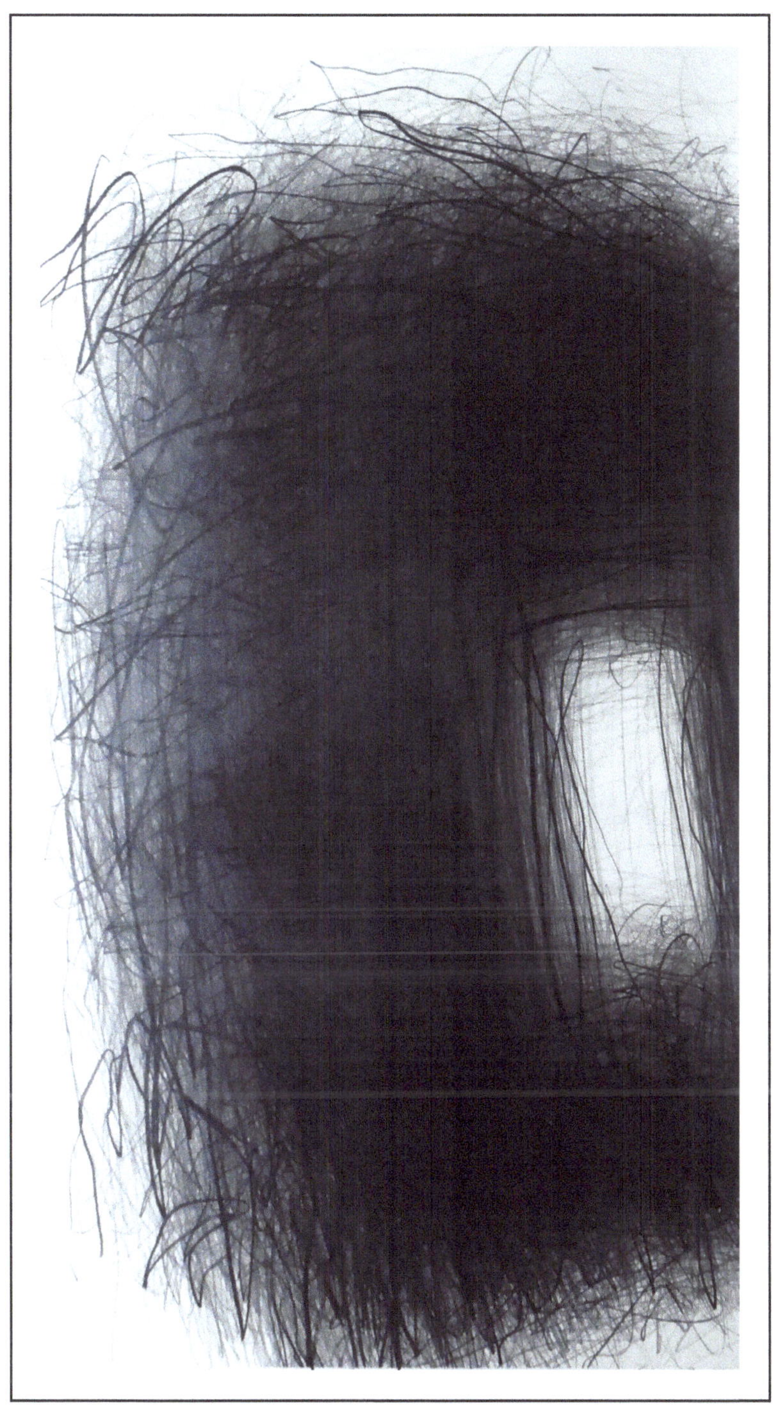

Desire

Scripture, television, Congress
Never quite alleviate our predicament.
Unresolved, it is embarrassing.
Biology, romance, circumstance,
I do not necessarily choose desire
For a particular man or woman.
Simply, I know this: the curve
Of your topography is appealing,
Your turns unsettling, your wit,
Your alchemy, a mystery of skin
Sheathing clockwork, mechanics
Of blood, bone, ligament, beguiling.
A man, my mind, too often myopic,
A thick, sticky mud sucking at boots,
I forget that we are still creatures,
Occasionally, clumsily, thrust
Together, panting, limbs splayed
For another, molecules bartered
In the nature of ecstasy, animals
Relinquishing our singularity,
Our bodies, fugacious perimeters,
Our instinct, illusions of continuation.
However random and primitive
Our desire, I admit, I find pleasure
In your company.

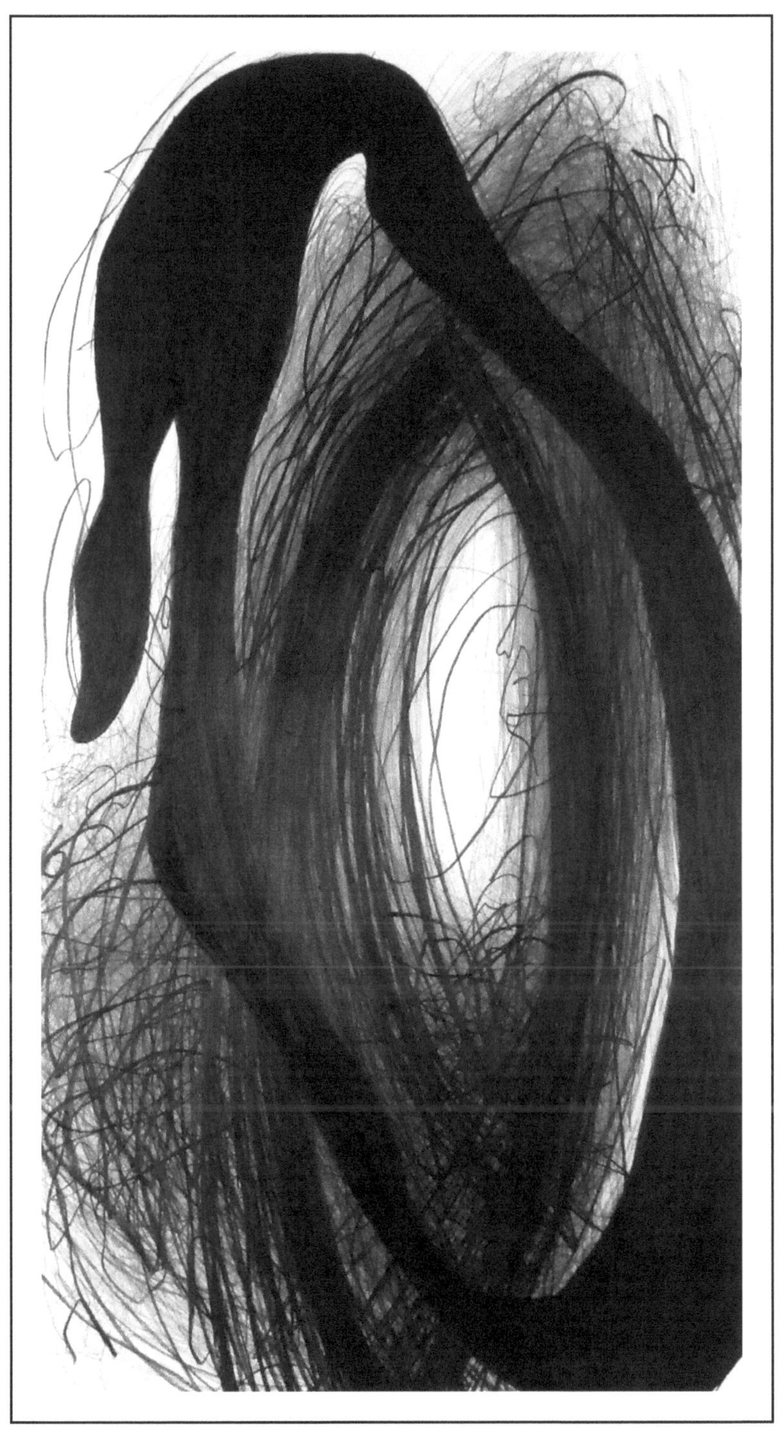

Just Boys

We were just boys,
Innocent in the eyes,
Yet hairless chests,
Half-naked, heedless
Woodland fauns
Sinning in God's sight,
Damned once, I suppose.

I took you in,
A soft puppy's head.
We laughed,
And that-was-that,
No-harm-done,
All-in-good-fun.

If we recalled,
If we divulged,
Confessed, unless
Their eyes betrayed them,
Our wives would be more
Thoughtful than shocked.
We were just boys.

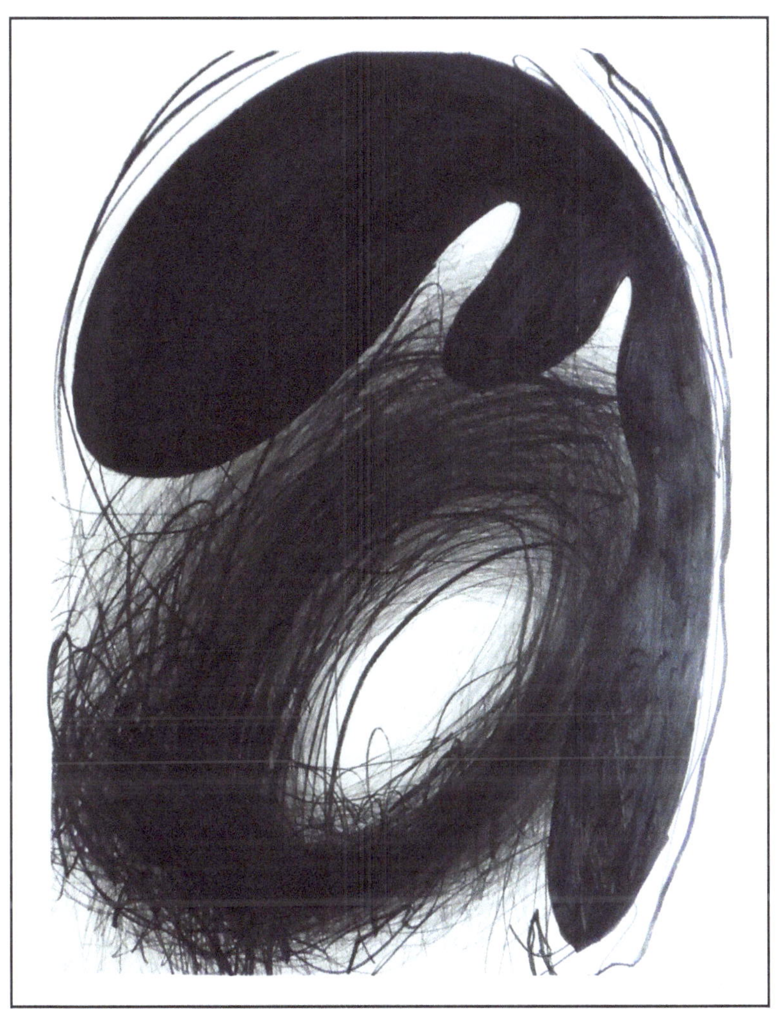

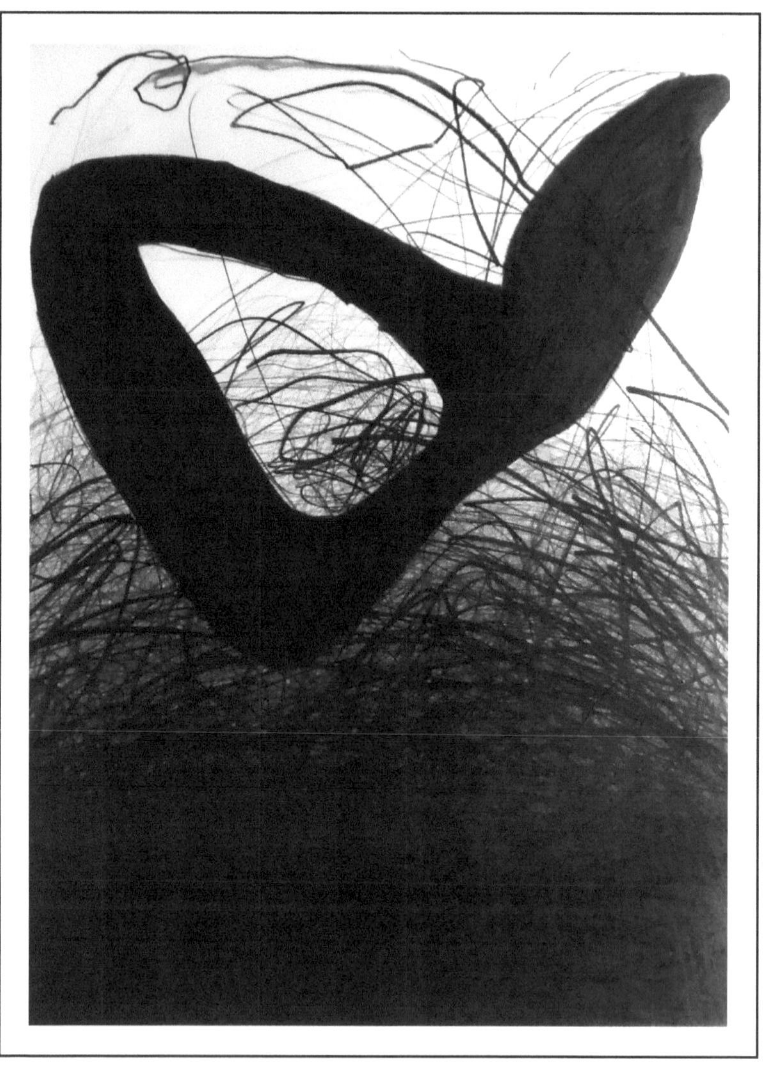

The Hip

I know this curve,
Often my obsession,
This supple turn.
I know this hip
In the night,
In the fog of sleep.
I know this crest,
Rising beside me,
Could be my own,
Narrow skeleton,
But she spreads wider,
A woman, her plain
A continent between
Summits. A passage
From belly to thigh
Surfaces upward against
Her skin, an eruption
Of stone against loam.
I could be blind,
My fingers charting
Familiar topography,
Reassuring contour.
I reminisce on this ridge,
A vast panorama:
Her hip pressing
My bones, a desire—
Her sacred ilium,
Cradled our babies.

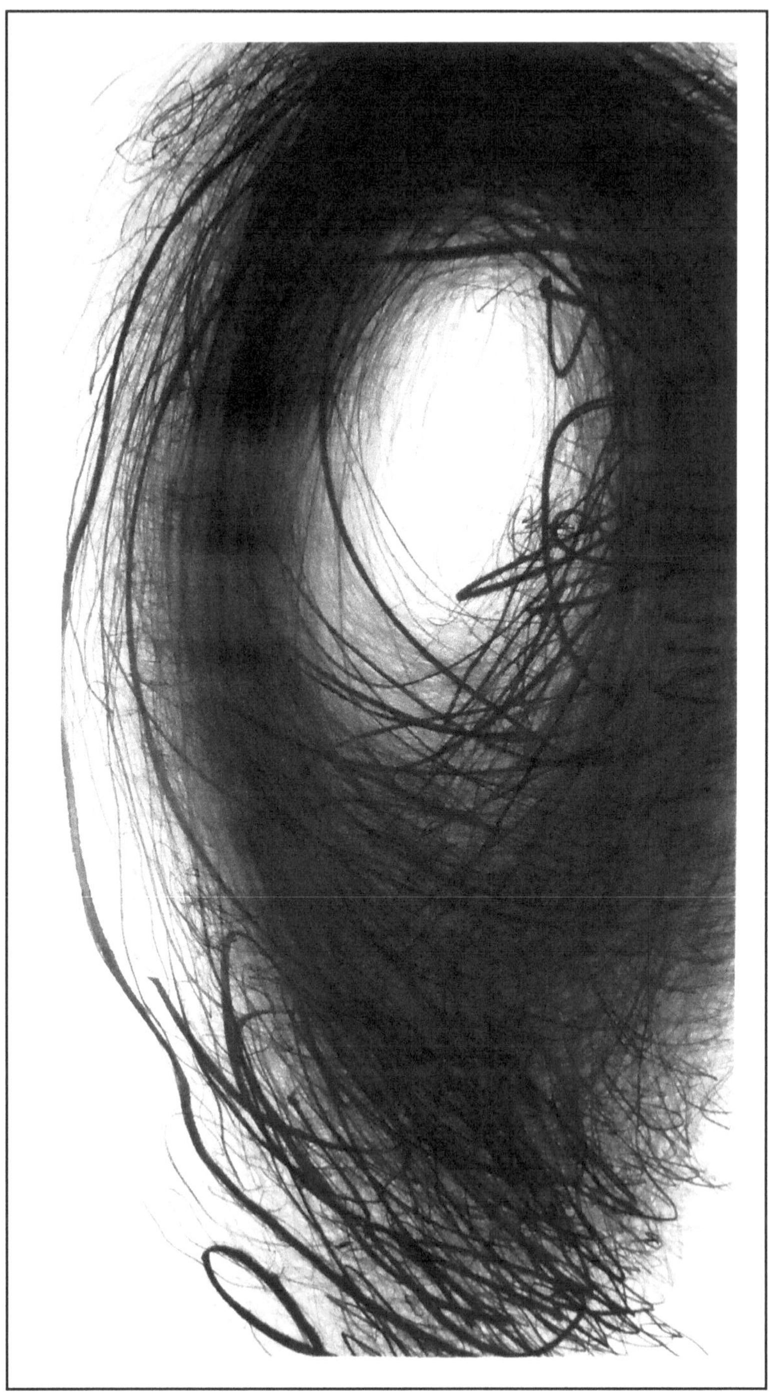

Ocean

Emily at two or three,
strapped in her car seat,
thoughtfully peers out the window
as we roll over Ohio hills,
the onset of Appalachia,
and exclaims, "The ocean, the ocean!"
as if the ocean were the culmination,
the expectation, of any long trip.

Foolishly, I attempt to explain
atmospheric perspective—
how the air is exceedingly heavy
with dust, heat and moisture,
turning the hills a vivid blue.
She's quiet, reflective for a while
then deciding, adamant, states,
"It is such a pretty ocean!"

Though now lashed to the mast,
I'll captain this vessel,
turn the tiller round, set sail,
plunge headlong into the waves.
We'll discover secret, pristine
beaches on distant islands,
marvel over exotic fishes,
delight in whales and dolphins.

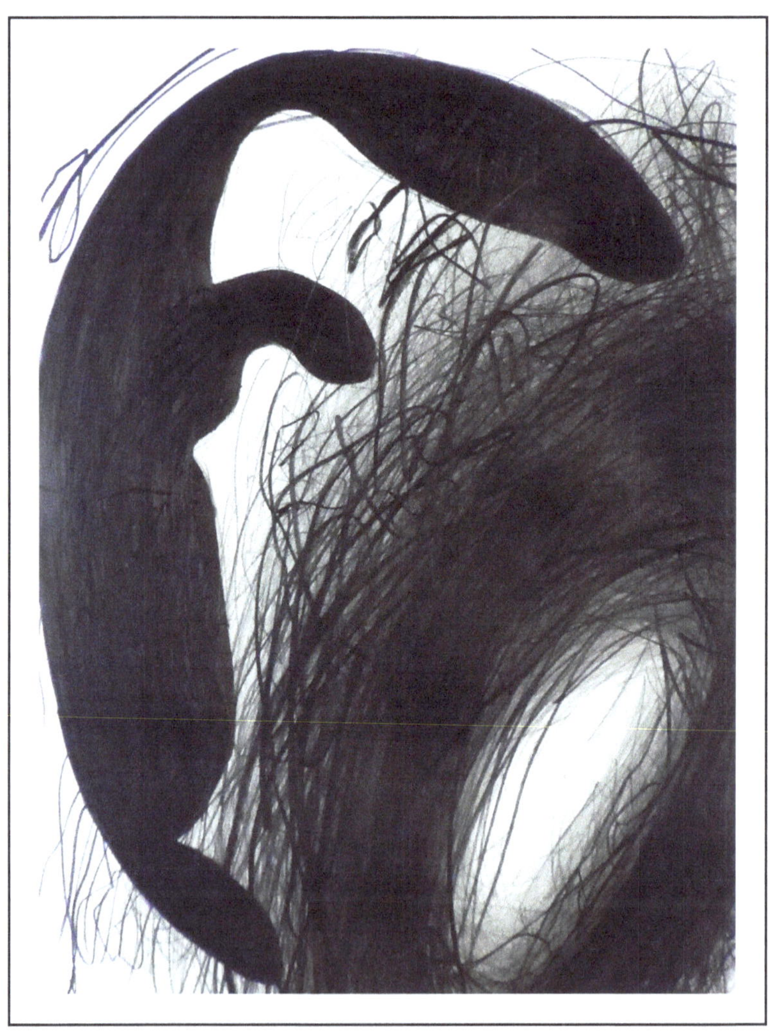

Reacquainted

I know this man,
now much taller than me,
who has his own life working,
biking, loving in the city.

It was last summer,
all of us together again
along the stunning granite
coast of Ogunquit, Maine.

It wasn't at the ocean shore,
Perkin's Cove, the Marginal Way,
the quirky, delicious tapas place,
Smokey Joe's Café on Broadway,
or one of many T-shirt shops.

Before breakfast, I watched
him sleep just so, exactly
as when he was a little boy,
arm curled above his head,
fingers lightly touching his brow.
I know this boy.

I Carry Love

I carry love on my back,
Riding high on spine and scapula.
Oh no, it's not what you think.
Love is never a burden. I am not
Usually bent from love's weight.
Very practically, I want love handy.
There are days when I sling it
From my shoulder to give it a look,
To wonder over its dimensions,
Love's beauty, love's intricate design
(And, obsessively, as a reassurance).

I would never abandon love
At the side of the road, on the
Church steps, in the grocery
Store, in produce or frozen foods.

However, a man, I can never
Carry love as so many do,
Cradled in my womb,
Love an intuitive knowing,
Love as natural, as constant as breath.
No, love abides outside me.
If I carried love somewhere between
Stomach and liver, I'm certain
I'd forget love's existence.
I'd construct presumptions.
If I hid love there, my fear
Of its loss would destroy me.

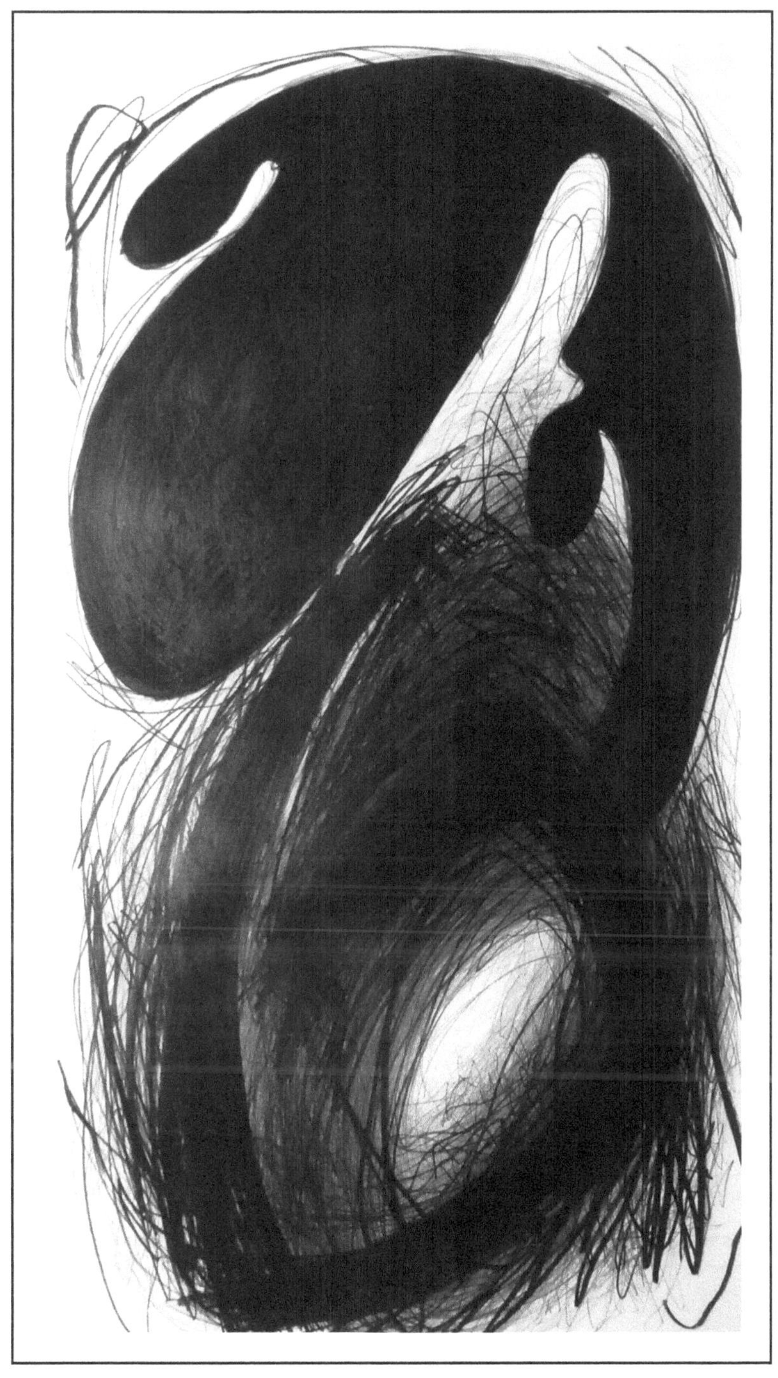

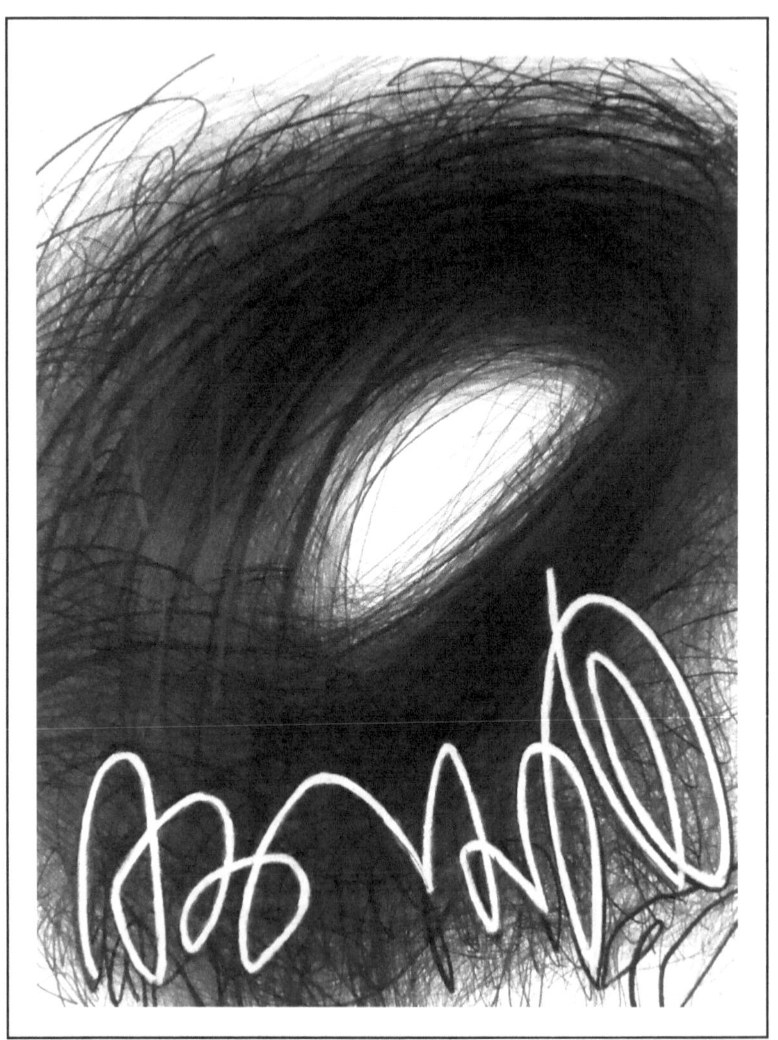

Cogs

We're eager to assume
Buttress our delusion
We're not mere cogs
Our lives not mechanical
We're unique and spontaneous
Charmingly eccentric on occasion
However we get up eat
Oil our gears watch the news
Accrue the years and conspire
With our vast machine
We fabricate we purchase
Obscenely we devour
Perversely we queue up
For the assembly line
For the check-out line
Our voracious bellies
Filled spilling sloppily
In plastic and metal things
Packaged in crisp edges
We're so clever
Our products witty
All for our convenience
Certainly there is a pleasure
When anything functions
When a wrench grips
And turns a bolt just so
And yet we're eager to assume
Our love-making is not mechanical
Our thrills unique and spontaneous
Our hips and sighs something
More than efficient pistons

Split

Uncle Gregg was split
In two, nearly two feet,
Cleaved down the center.
Though curious,
Everyone was too polite.
Of course, I asked.

He lifted his shirt above
Belly and breast,
A gracious, intimate nakedness,
But he was eager to reveal,
Prove our inevitability,
Our mortality. Look! See?

His scar, a vertical wry smile,
Nearly a grimace, laughed
At me, opened his heart to me.
I've heard survivors say
After this surgery, only
Matters of love are significant.

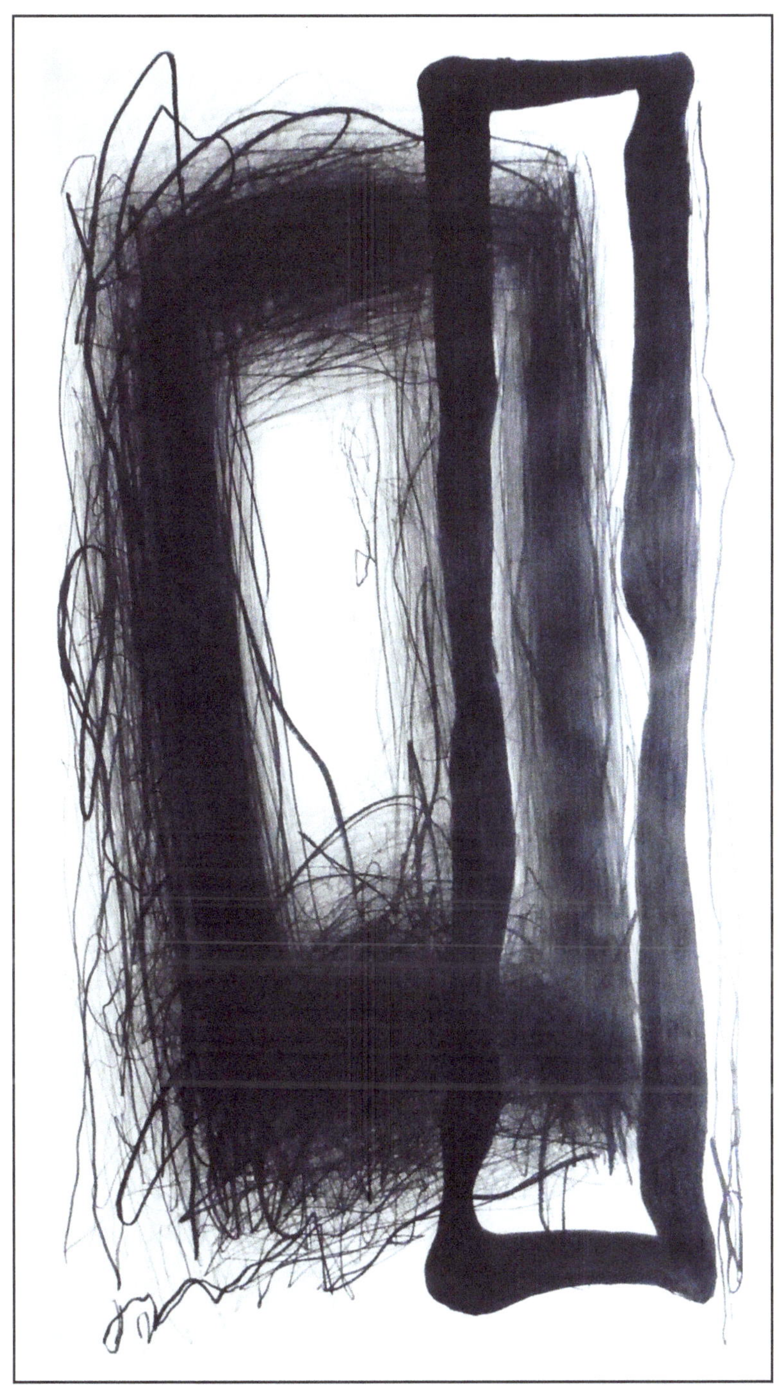

Imperfection

A while ago, a doctor
Measured my heartbeat
And declared it failed
To operate as most
Other men and women,
Its peaks and depressions
Too high, too deep,
Unusual in its thumping.
"That sounds about right,"
I said, conceding my flaw,
And proceeded to think
Nothing of the verdict.

Just recently, Lisa, the nurse,
A nice young woman
Whom I made laugh
A little, took a scan,
A picture of my belly,
And caught another fault
At the very hub of me,
My thrombosis, my obstacle.
It might have been more
Telling if she simply poked
At my middle with her finger
And said, "There, right
There, is your imperfection,
The source of your suffering."

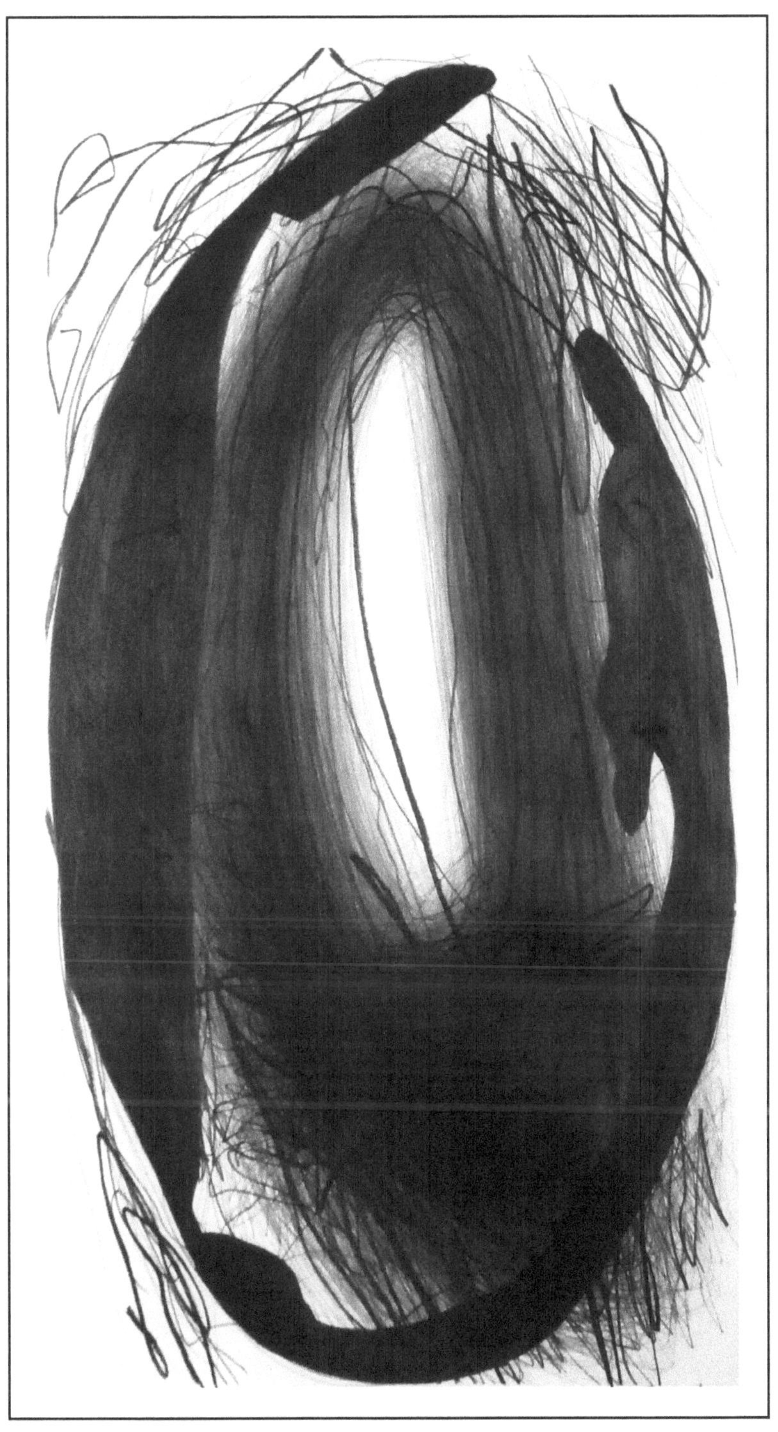

Aria

Not once have I wept over art in the Louvre, Uffizi or Met.
Well, almost over van der Weyden's *Descent* in the Prado,
Mary's grief, but that may have been indigestion after
Madrid's tapas, the Museum of Ham. A lithograph
in Chelsea, Kathe Kollwitz's dead mother and child splayed,
stiff, discarded on the curb, brought a single, quiet tear.

At the reception, the gallery on Water Street, I am at first
preoccupied with drawings, paintings, prints, porcelain;
delicate, curious assemblages, diminutive Constructivism;
with wine, cheese and those gooey sweets with coconut,
marshmallows, and caramel; with the hot breath
of claustrophobic conversation. In a corner, a soprano,
hired for the evening, presses "play" for her boombox
accompaniment. Unexpectedly, the press of gawkers
hushed, from this spare, pretty young woman an aria.

At my age, too cynical or circumspect, on most days,
I assume nothing may move me so again, but with her voice,
sobs come suddenly, exquisitely pure, crystalline tears.
All pretense and pettiness fall away. Instantly, this moment
is beauty. I am *Saint Teresa in Ecstasy,* her voice piercing
me with divinity. However skeptical my arrogant past, this,
at last this, must be God's love.

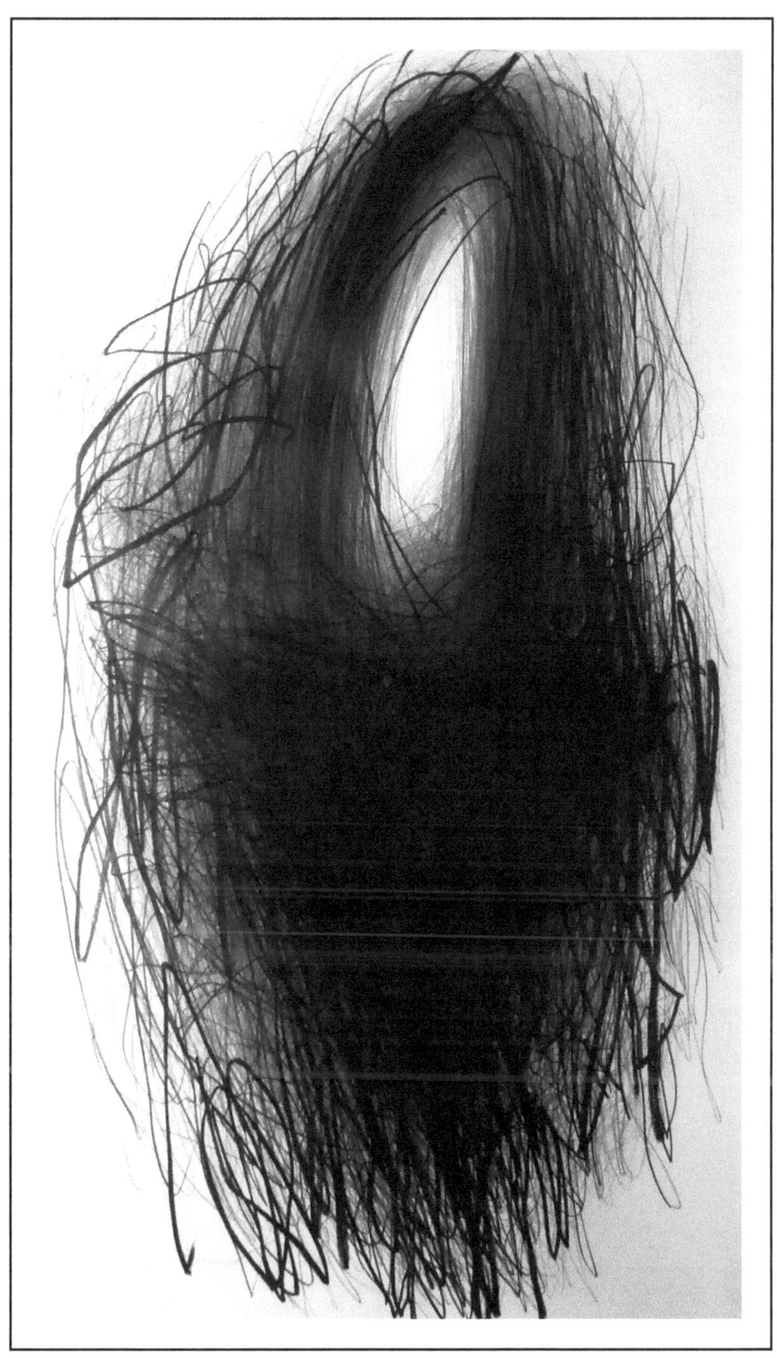

Constructivism

The girl, a novice pipefitter, who drove a pickup, shunned
high heels, and attempted to correct her grammar (but not
so much as the effort seemed an unnecessary annoyance)
was acquainted with exceedingly rectilinear Russians,
Malevich, Tatlin, Gabo, and the German Dada Schwitters
who proclaimed to Richter in a café, "I am an artist and
I nail my pictures together."

She and I hung her painting, her tryst with Constructivism,
her colors crisp and potent like green, yellow and red
peppers at the end of summer. And in our task, incidentally,
innocuously, I brushed her arm, the underside of her limb,
her antithesis of assemblage, that downy, tender place,
her curve, still vulnerably feminine between the hinges
of elbow and wrist, where grit and sun often missed.

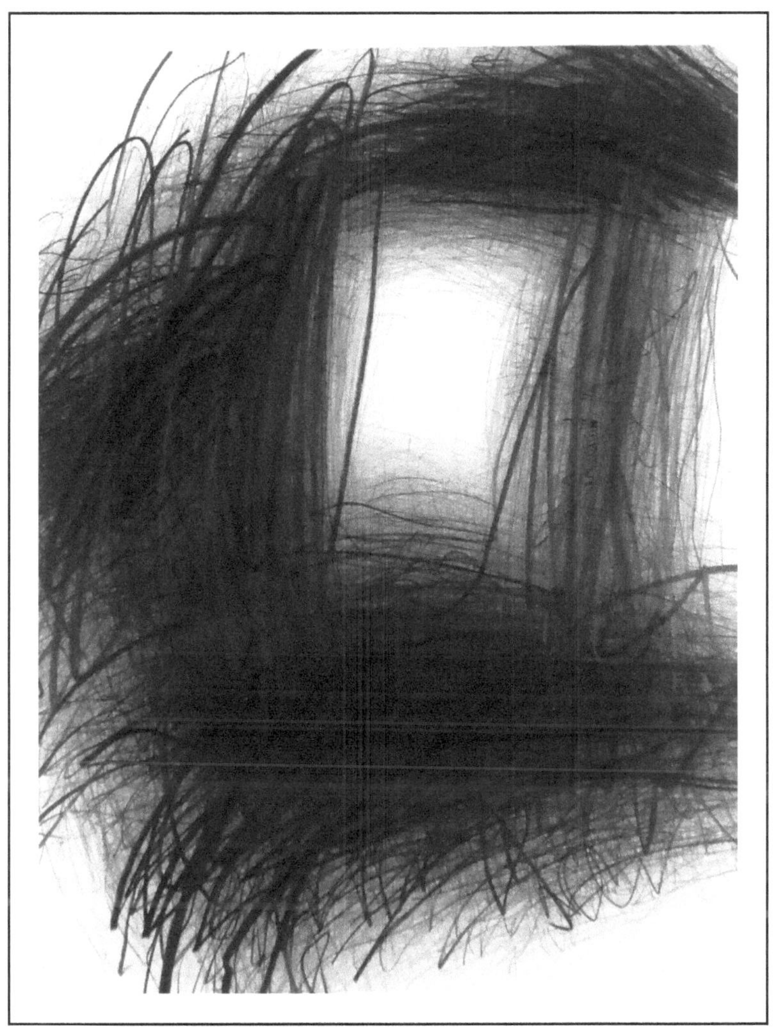

Canada

Now I comprehend
Our heady summer
So long ago somewhere
Star Wars buzzing about
Above our heads swatting
Ronny and Maggie posturings
Despite preordained preferences
(We pined for exquisite vulvas
Symmetry and pinkishness)
We wanted we wanted
I wanted to kiss you
Without assessing your lips
(Now there's something!)
We burned melted
Into one (the sun!)
We squeezed the air
A plump red teat
In O Canada!
My gawd that meadow
The lucerne a seductive emerald
We sprawled we crushed
Violet alfalfa blossoms
Our smooth flat chests
Giddy as little girls' first
Infatuation a redolence
Of newly planed lumber
Disinclined to regard nipples
You a fair downy Saxon
Me a dark barbarian from
Swarthy steppes ancestors
Two desperate for desire
We made do with love.

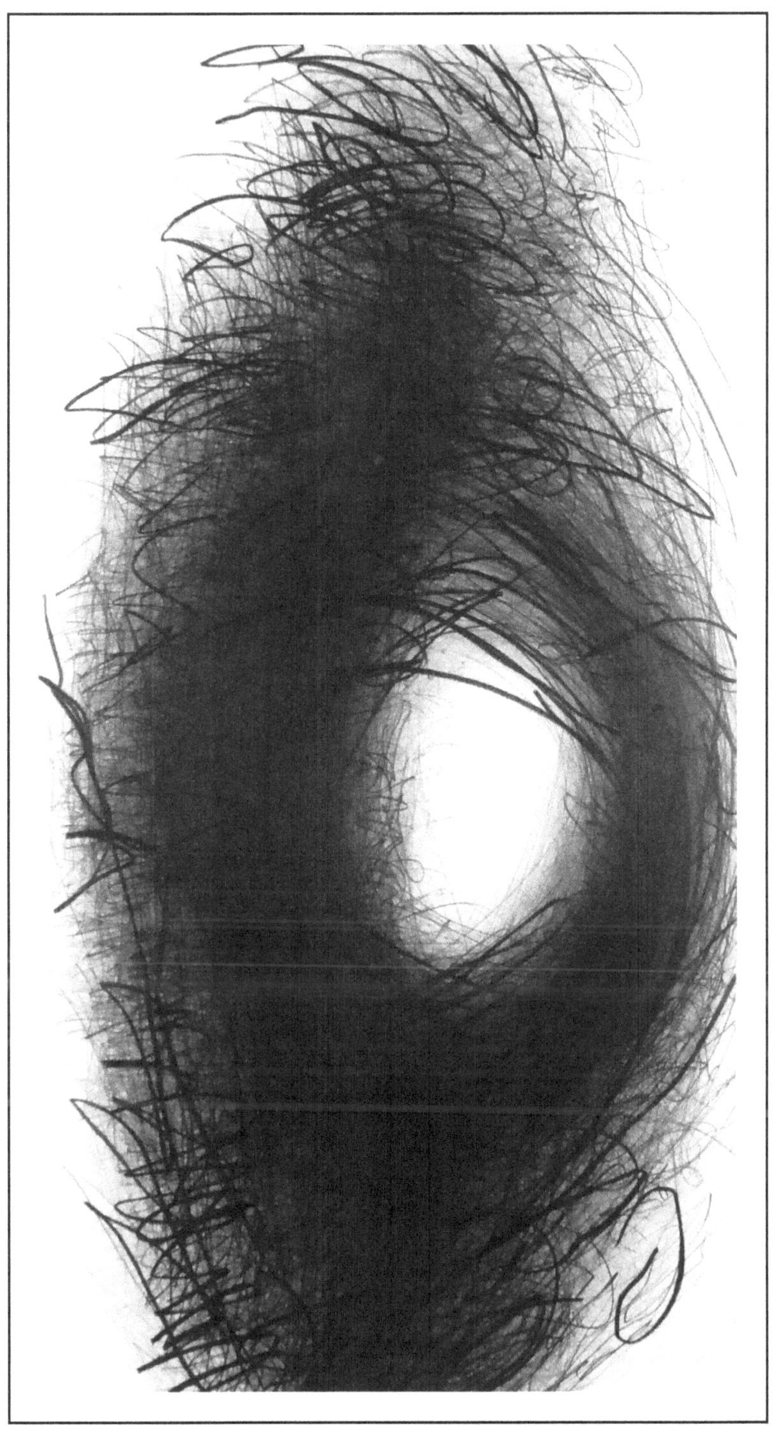

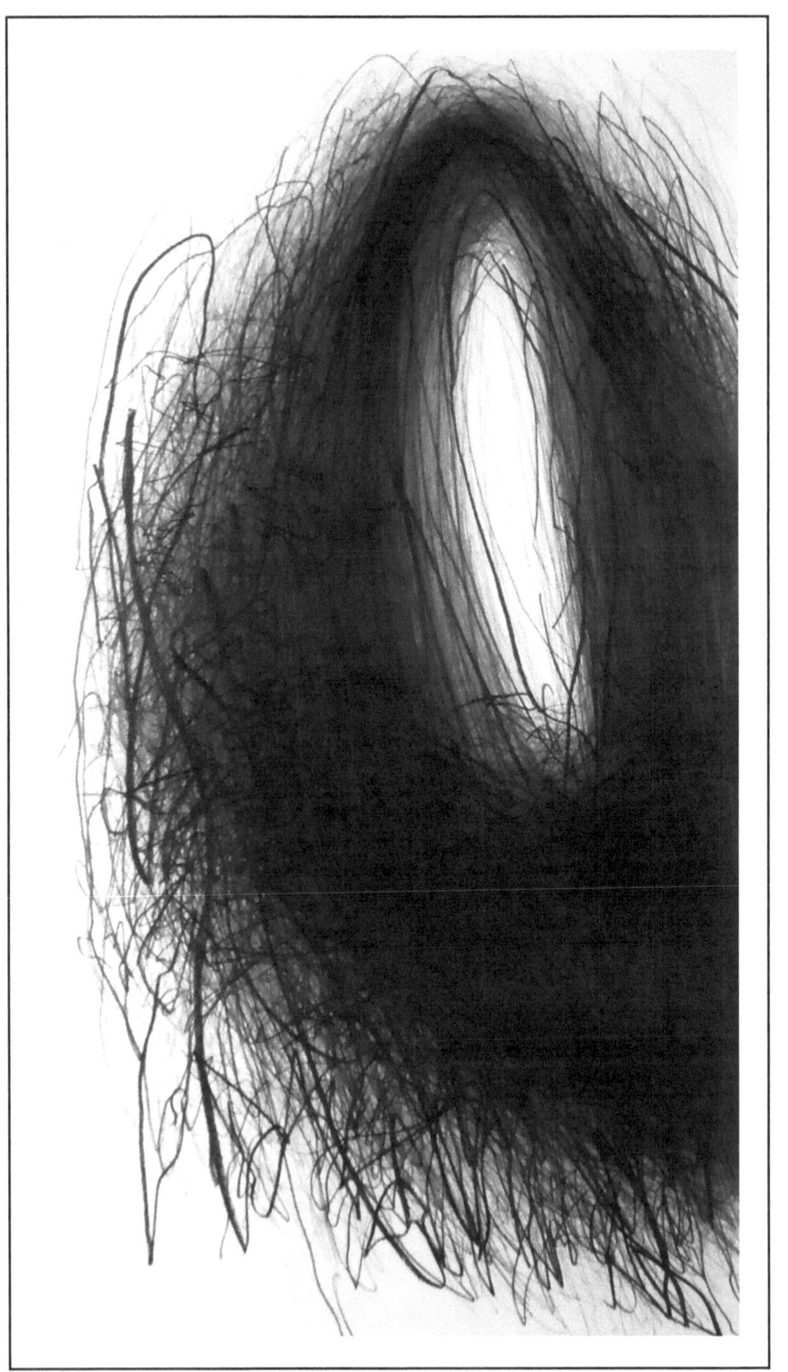

A Monk

I shall be a monk, ambitious Benedict, aspiring bodhisattva.
I will reckon my days in obsessive breviary, lauds, vespers,
nocturns, thumbing a rosary, spinning a prayer wheel.

My feet will tread on cool stone, dim abbey nave, or in
warm, golden stupas. In the scriptoria, my pen will scratch
at lined, illuminated parchment, but I will renounce noise,

the habitual din, silence my new scripture. I will don
a saffron robe, offer my empty bowl at the supermarket.
Holy beggar? Alms? Well, no, my backyard is my cloister,

a suburban ranch blessed with every convenience, TV,
washer-dryer, microwave. I will embrace obscurity,
zealously relish isolation. Will I dwell upon Buddha,

or will I simply gaze upon descending blossoms, infinite
petals, spring? And look! Now winter, apples, irrevocably
frozen, still cling to bare limbs, still red, beguile the deer.

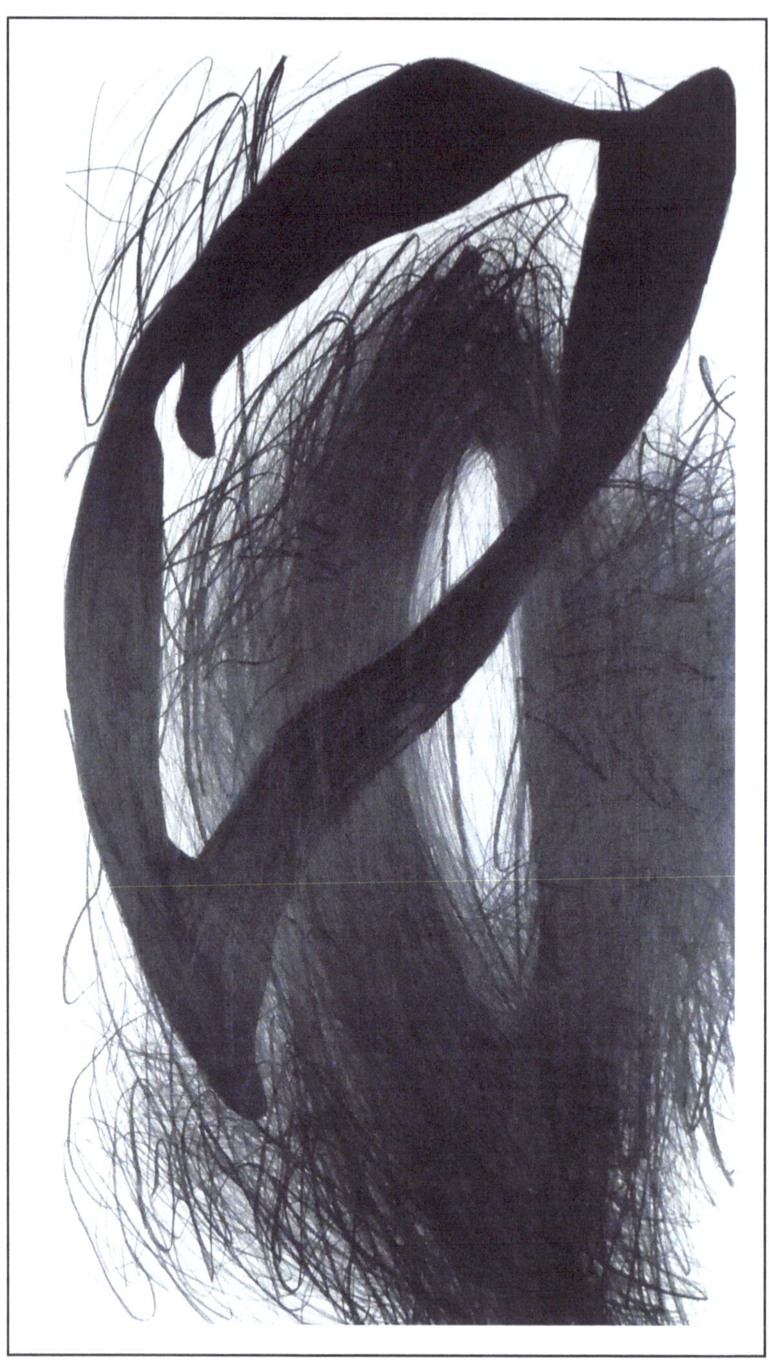

Master and Pupil

When he was a young man, an earnest but nutty art
student, Charles Robert came to my door painted
head-to-toe in Ultramarine Blue, seeking advice
and turpentine. Even then, he could have been a blue
Krishna wooing Radha.

Now colleagues, he is the swami, and I remain, as ever,
the professor. (Too attached to my role, perhaps it's time
to return to apprentice.) Distinctions between master and
pupil blur when we're equally forgiving of imperfections,
of clumsy hierarchy, of the tally of infinite karma.

Now he resides in Thailand, blissfully lost in a forest
of stupas. And I remain lost, burrowed in Ohio, suburbia,
a plastic illusion. I wonder how our routines differ.
The Pacific between us, he has his meditation; I have
my television.

Now, tonight, I apprehend, from separate continents,
a modest nirvana. We pine over the same horizon.
We desire the same moon, the curve of an alms bowl,
the color of monks' robes, a delicious, saffron crescent
set thoughtfully in a blue-black sky, a slice of melon—
no, a peach placed on Krishna's belly.

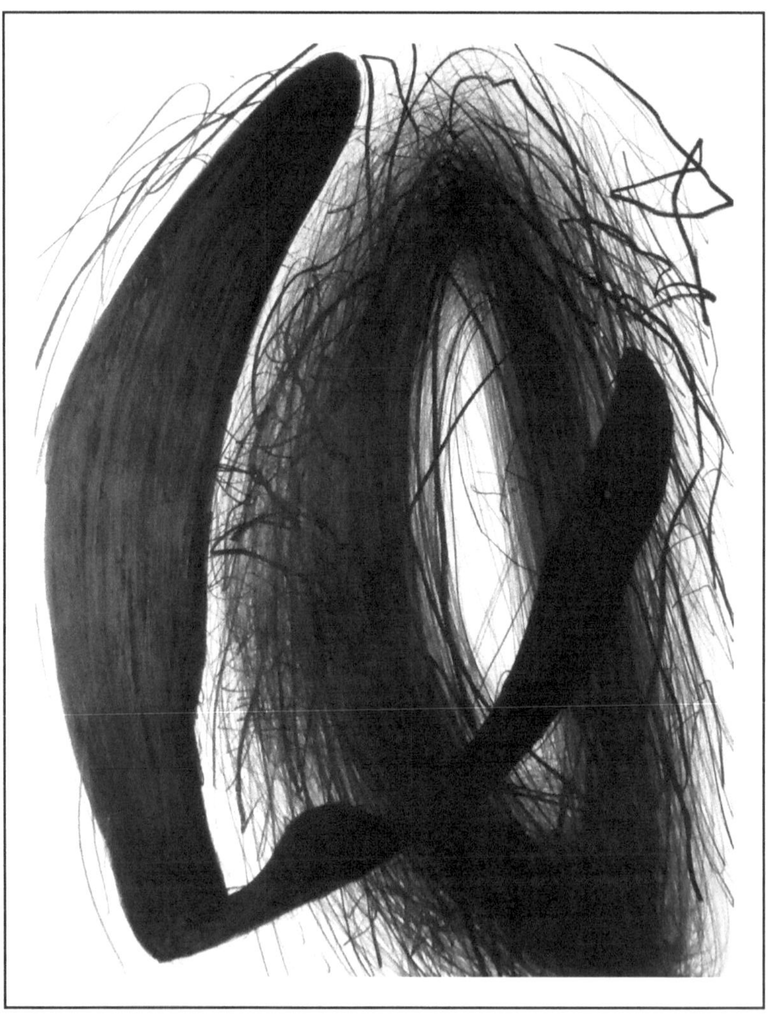

Young Siddhartha

A small statue of Siddhartha Gautama sits cross-legged on my desk. His smile is serene; however, my prayer wheel stopped spinning when I dwelled on this: Siddhartha, the prince, wanted for nothing and saw nothing. His smile was serene behind tall, gleaming palace walls at the foot of the Himalayas, where the air was cold and thin until, on a stroll, he felt the soil of his kingdom beneath his feet, rather than smooth, colorful tile, thick, rich carpet—until his desire to comprehend an old man, a corpse, and a beggar.

At twenty-nine, Siddhartha left his princess, sheer silks and gold bangles sliding on her hips but no bliss, no enlightenment in the curve of her arms. Her serene smile, her lips, her dark nipples, the color of earth and dates, would not hold him. Siddhartha left his infant boy, Rahula, after dubbing him "little fetter," wriggling karmic manacle, his son's serene smile a tether. At thirty-five, after six years and two gurus, his empty ribs unsatisfied with ascetic life (Was all that near-death necessary?), he knew, however hobbled, he could return to his father's table.

After forty-nine days and nirvana—finally no crying baby—Siddhartha found his serene smile under the leaves and figs of the Bodhi tree, the Buddha, an open, white lotus floating above the mud. And yet he did not return to his wife and son. It occurred to me, now twenty years older than the Buddha, perhaps Siddhartha was simply a naive and foolish young man. Oh, what an exquisite flaw! My smile is serene. At eighty, the Buddha concluded, his smile fixedly serene, he mastered the shackles of his samsara, the endless, dizzy spin of birth and death. Maybe, just maybe, Siddhartha might have gone round again.

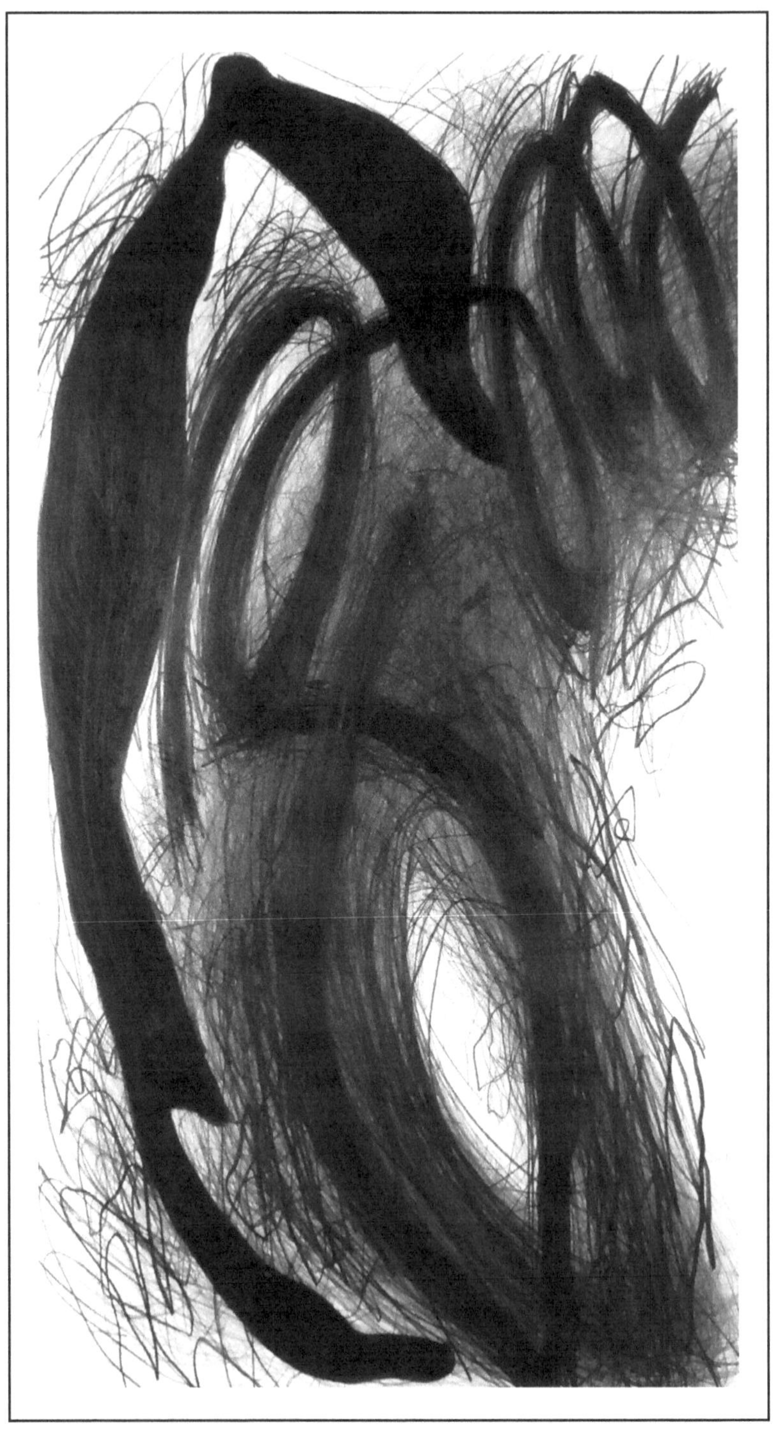

The Artist

I happened upon a line
In the snow, an intrepid mouse
The scribe, a chronicle of his
Expedition across the Arctic,
But more expression than map,
Not one harsh, mathematical angle,
A beautiful, intentional meandering.
I assumed I was the artist,
My lines drawn across a white
Expanse and hung in galleries
For admiration or, at the very least,
Thoughtful consideration, a faulty illusion.
The mouse was a little Leonardo.
No, his line was Zen calligraphy,
A monk choreographing
The length of a scroll in ink,
Brush as wide as a hand.
More akin to Expressionism,
Random marks of inner necessity,
de Kooning or Gorky were the fit.
With a branch I set out to mimic
The mouse arabesque.
None of these were adequate,
None as exquisite as the master.

In the Snow

I regret neglecting
The egrets last summer
Mindlessly oblivious to
White against emerald
Viridian chartreuse
Stepping shyly in the marsh
And just yesterday
Snowing and snowing
I wish I'd spent
An afternoon peering
Through the window
(Debussy in my ears no
A Chopin Mazurka)
Blue-gray atmosphere
Obscurity on the horizon
A sky brimming with
Falling singularities more
Crystals than space between
I knew this beauty
Was infinitely transient
Considerably more pertinent
Than fabricating drudgery
My bloated memoranda
Tell me tell me
(I do not insist
A modest desire
A desperation nevertheless)
There must be a place
Where I might see
Egrets taking flight
In the snow

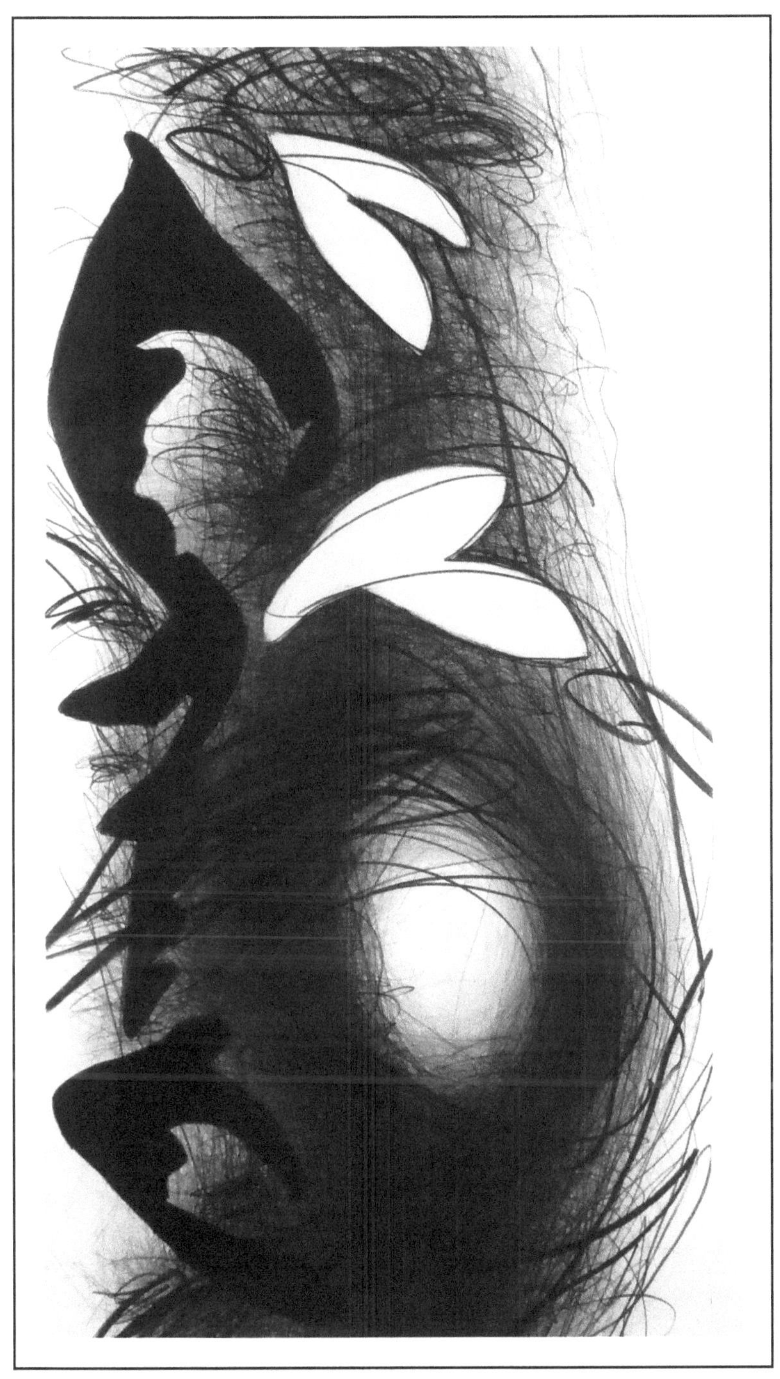

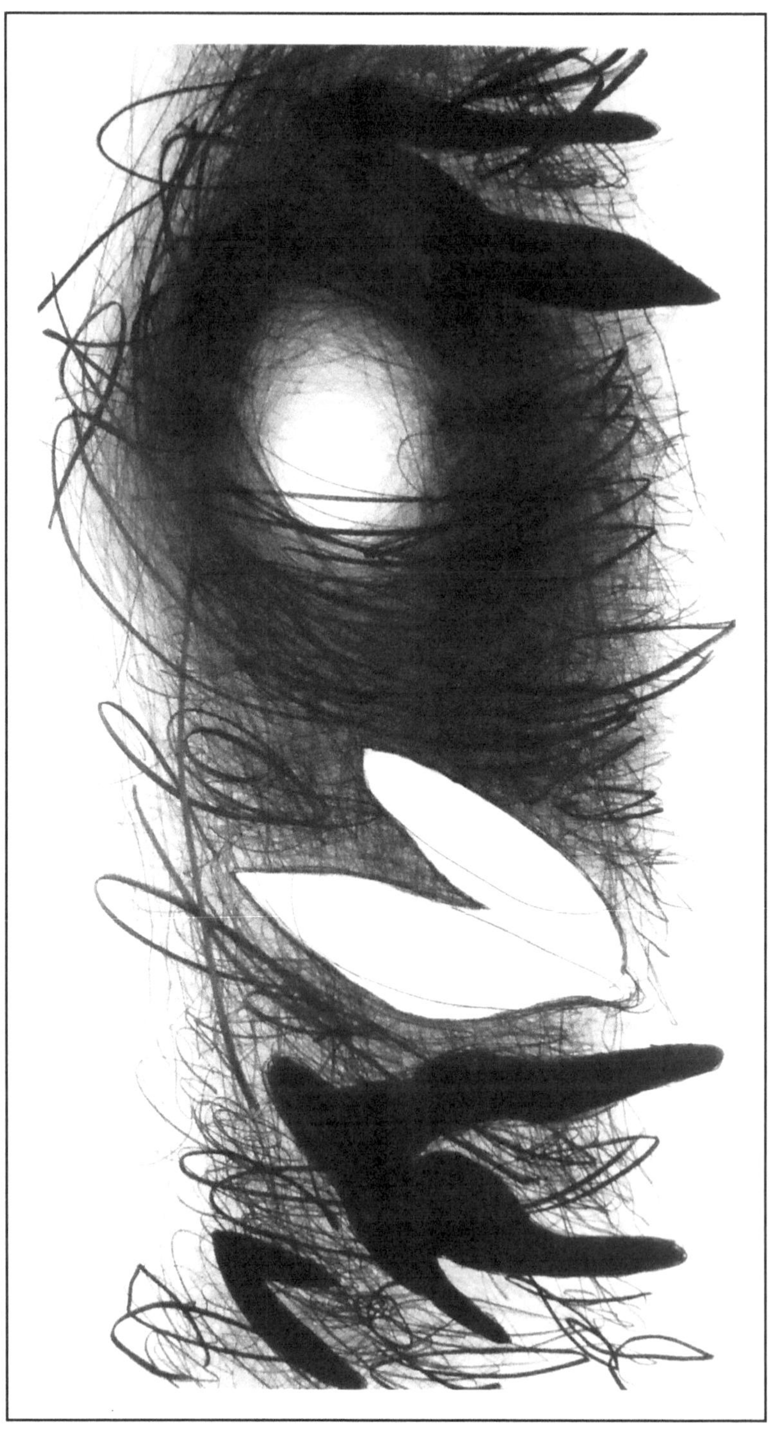

A Saffron Moon

A saffron moon
Elusive exotic orange hue
The dye of monks' robes lingers
Suspended this morning on the
Horizon's wrist of emerald
And blue-gray eyes of distant hills
I know this full ripe fruit
Will slip from the sky's lip
But for a moment I am duped
I presume this moon this color
This instant was ceded only to me
It will fit nicely in my pocket
Though speculators scheme and
Surveyors ogle through lenses no one
May own the Sea of Tranquility
Now the saffron moon hovers in the east
Above the *Great Buddha's* brow
Its reflection illuminates
Radiant golden domed stupas
Now the eyes of any caste may
Merely gaze upward to possess
A saffron moon

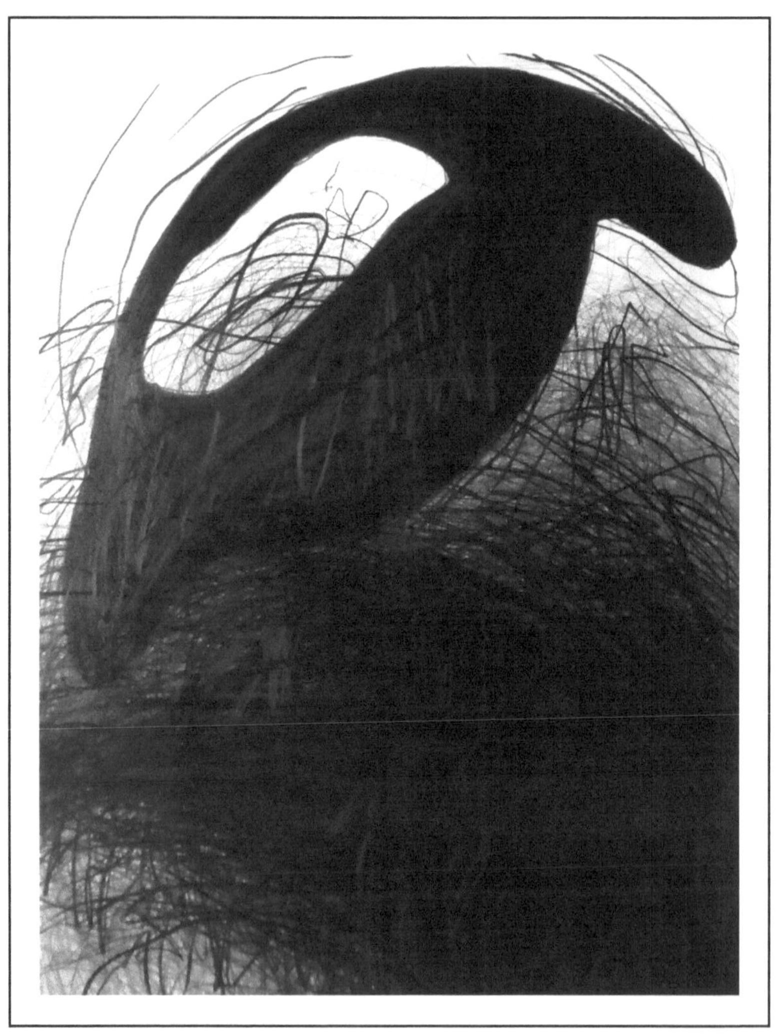

A Vision

I cannot deny it, a vision
(As much as I am prone
To visions which is not usually).
Old Woman Creek arrives
On my left from a primordial,
Underground origin, sliding over
Pastures, carving steep ravines
Through woods, then departs on my right,
Relinquishing all form, its identity,
In the wide estuary of Lake Erie.
Lao Tzu's *Watercourse Way*
Flows through the middle of me,

My body, two flat stones,
A sluice for all manner of flotsam,
Everything significant and trivial
Continuously coming and going.
I apprehend your doubt.
I am skeptical as well.
This vision, not quite hallucination,
Not quite apparition, likely
An impractical indulgence,
Is a tiny ecstasy, a little
Trickle of nirvana, a potent,
Essential illusion, nonetheless.

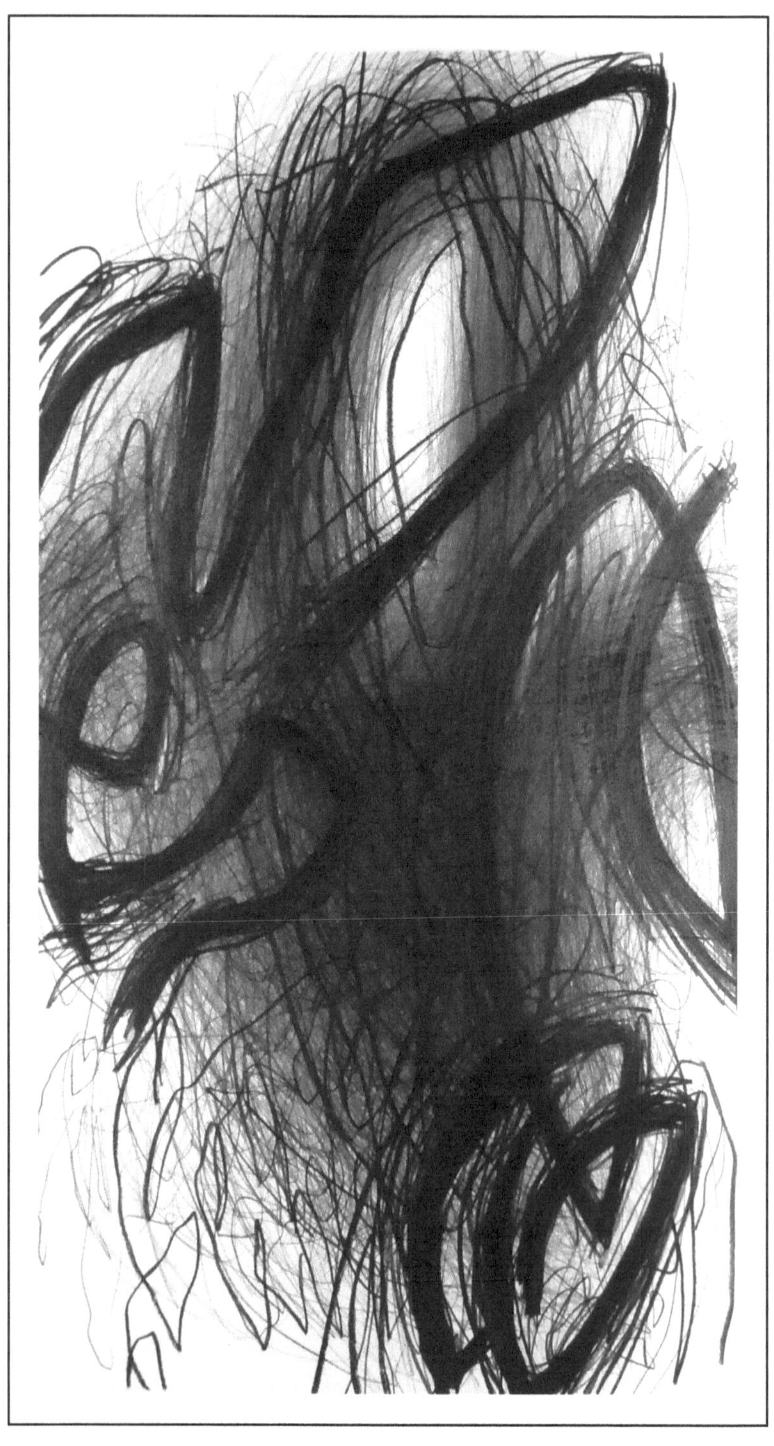

The Watercourse Way

I didn't listen when, a very long time ago, Lao Tzu
and Siddhartha matter-of-factly, kindly informed me that
the chaos of my mind is likely the origin of my suffering,
my worry, my obsession or rather my attempt to harness
it is my madness.

Eventually, painfully, I discovered my mind is not
fabricated of levers and gears, wires and switches.
It is a faulty analogy, a dreadful misconception, to view
my head as an oily machine or a set of circuits, to assume
there's an orderly schematic to apprehend, to follow.
My mind, my mind is as nature, moves as water
(the sage's *Watercourse Way*) and acts accordingly,
defying, pushing at artificial edges.

Occasionally my mind is routed by a pipe or canal.
However, dams and levees fail. To grab ahold of it
is a futile, illusive endeavor. So silly. As anyone,
from time to time I am damp with a few tears or
drenched in a sudden storm.

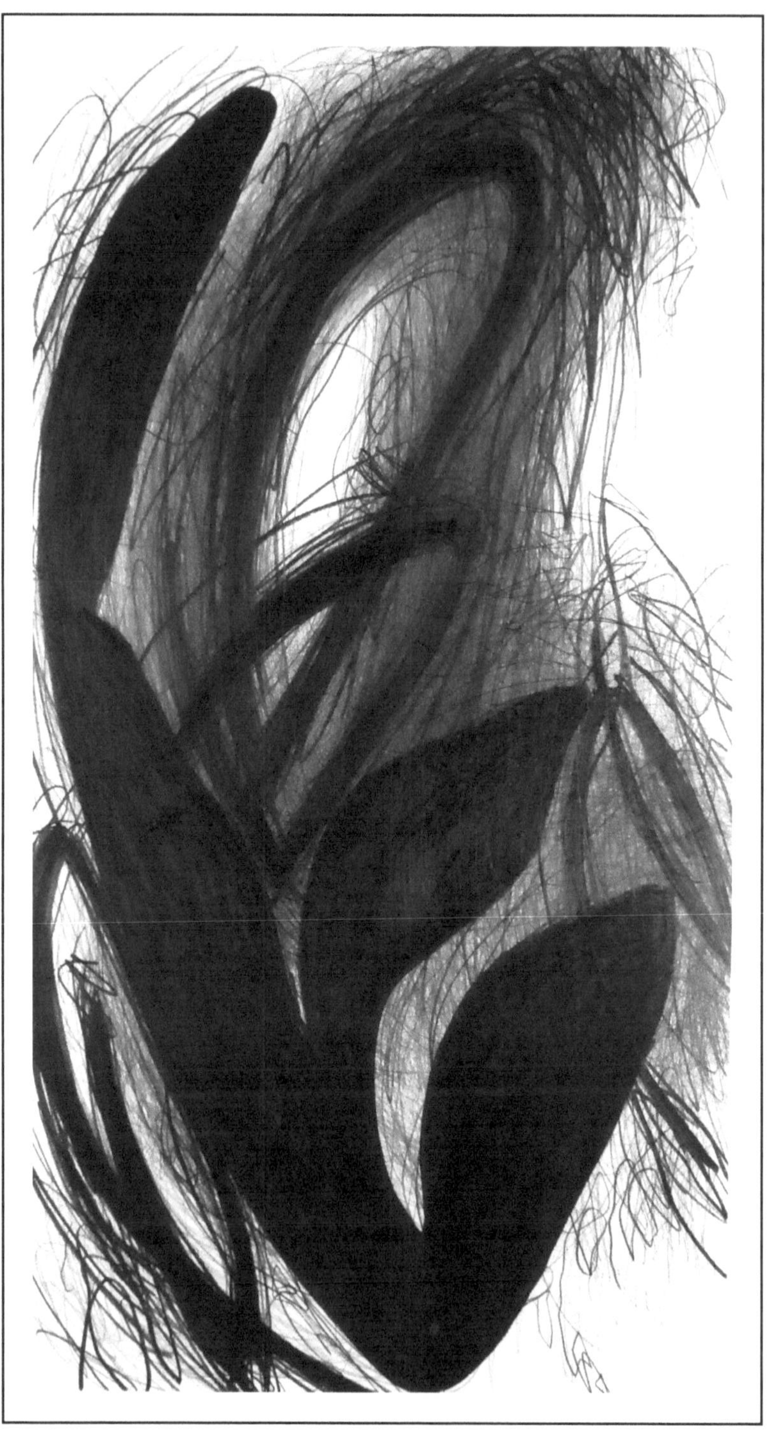

Laughing Buddha

On the little oxbow shelf along Old Woman Creek,
a bend I frequent now and then, there's a quiet,
contemplative spot, lush foliage and silent decay,
where I considered placing a statue of the laughing
buddha, one of those concrete casts, yard art found
on the corner of two country highways. I'd paint it
a bright pink, proof of my whimsy—oh gee,
spontaneous me. The idol would remind me
of suffering, three of four Noble Truths,
the elusiveness of nirvana, the futile pursuit
of absolutes. Obviously, the object would declare
that I was here and put it there. Or maybe an image
of the Virgin Mary or Saint Francis of Assisi would do,
popular icons on tidy suburban lawns. (A little
known martyr would express my hip penchant
for obscurity. Better yet, how about Uncle Wayne
or Mrs. Hennel, my second-grade teacher?)
If it were Mary, I would enjoy a perceptible increase
in mercy and a marked decline in despondency.
If Francis, I wouldn't meditate upon Saint or pope.
I'd recall Assisi, those exquisite Giotto frescos in the
basilica's upper chapel, the toy-like architecture,
the charming characters in dramatic tableaus.
Or I'd pine for that trattoria discovered around
the corner from the Roman temple, the pasta superb,
surpassing the usual tourist fare and worth the climb
up steep, uneven medieval alleys. On second thought,
any effigy remains out of the question.

Two Buddha

One hundred miles west of Kabul once stood two colossal buddha cut into a sandstone cliff when the slow, careening caravans of cloth, spices, opium, wine, and coin passed below on the Silk Road; when the sun was not too harsh, the pilgrims looked up, overwhelmed, and carried the Buddha's gaze to China.

So far from India, so far from the *Bo Tree at Gaya,* the monks who carved the icons, the beloved, hollowed out niches and abided beside the still ones, tending to their whims. And in our time, the refugees of war who sought solace there, puzzled at the frescos of angels painted above their heads.

When the Taliban, when Mullah Mohammad Omar decreed the false idols destroyed, explosions flung serene smiles into space; the sacred returned to the infinite grains of sand. The Buddha, now more than two at your feet, sift swiftly through the fingers. All that's left are empty silhouettes, shadows in the rock face.

From nations, scholars, and the devout arose an outcry. "Why?" But at last, after fifteen centuries, the Buddha, red in the face, laughs a big belly laugh; tears squirt from his eyes, and after he slaps his thigh and catches his breath shouts out, "*Anitya!* Perfect timing!"

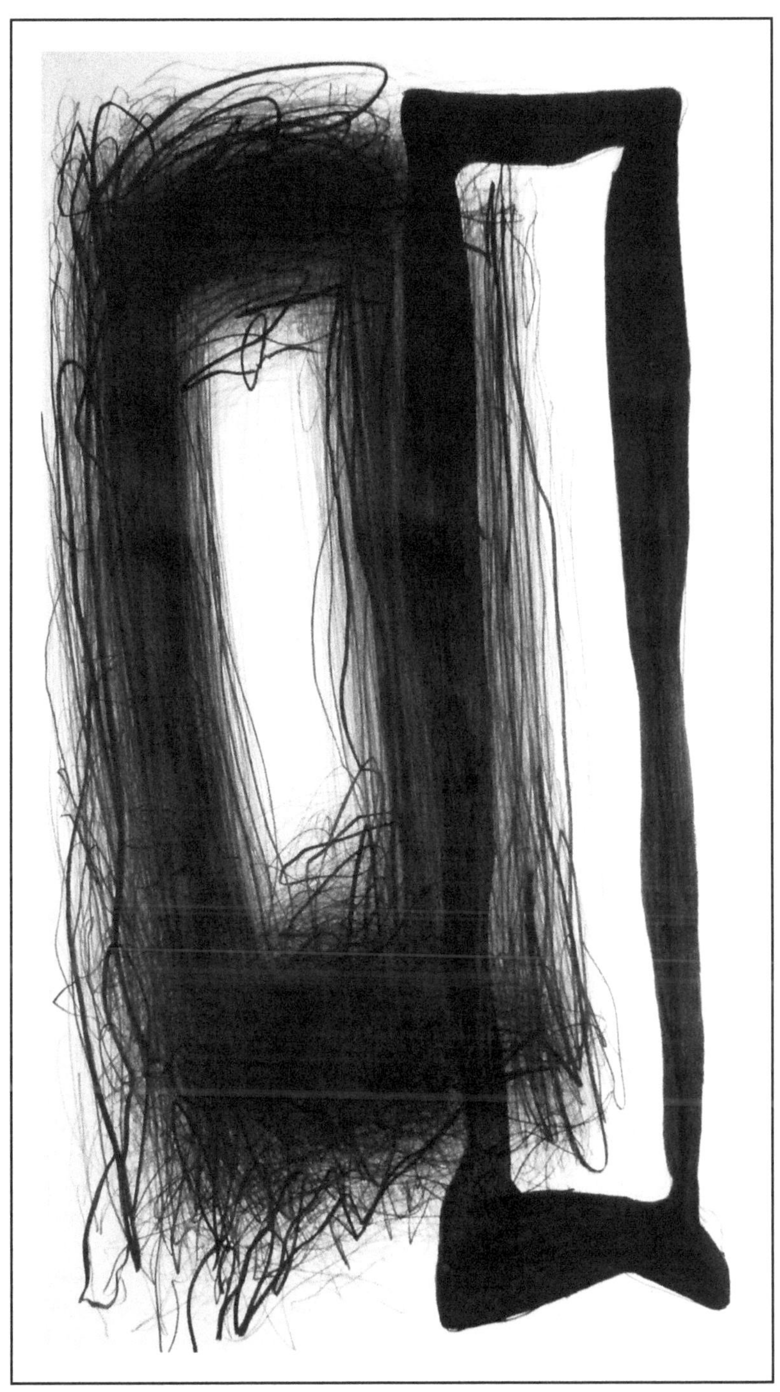

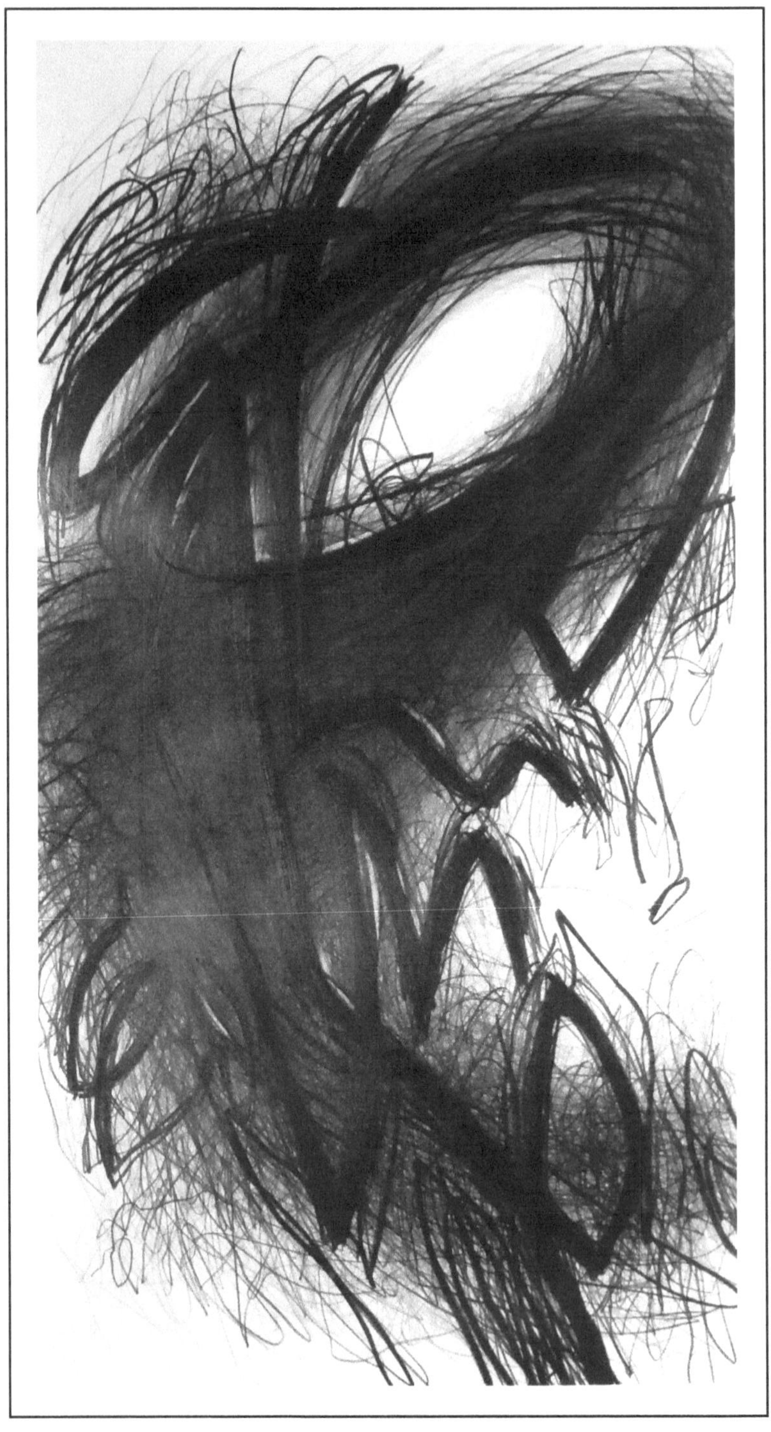

Paradise

In the beginning, Eden before Elysium, Satan the sly snake,
was actually God, slithering and hissing in masquerade.
Omniscient God had a hunch we'd screw it up. God,
a lousy parent, his original sin, his consequence, was simply
this: he knew the petulant Adam would throw a tantrum.
God laid it out for the thick-headed dolt. (Eve got it
immediately, even saw through God's quiz, but as usual,
we ignored her circumspection, her diffidence a disaster.)
God whispered in his ear, "You shall die one day. In this
beauty, in this garden, in your ignorance, your avarice,
you shall slowly destroy yourselves."

And we did so with perverse enthusiasm, with stones,
swords, bullets, then exquisitely sleek and efficient missiles.
We leveled mountain peaks for heat—presumptuous heights!
bulldozed and slathered it all with sticky asphalt, irrevocable
concrete; sawed forests to stumps for our pulp as we have
boundless and profound introspections to express, a spewing
of narcissism; dumped our sludge, filled our seas; heaped
our plastic islands to wield our omnipotence, our arrogance.
Dear Adam, how pungent was the fragrance, how seductive,
how sweet the fruit? Did your tongue come alive in
paradise? Or, in the end, did you merely articulate a pout?

We Fool Ourselves

We fool ourselves,
But the design,
The reality is simple.
Above, the vast
And capricious sky
Relents just beyond
Its blue, its tempests.
No north or south,
No up or down,
Galaxies spin and spin
Headlong into heavens.

Below, the earth
Is immutable,
Weighty and final.
True, its belly roils,
Brooding and terrible,
But we ignore this.
We're more acquainted
With its skin,
With sand, sharp cliffs,
With our mud, our heady,
Moldering loam.

In between, all
Is fragile illusion,
At best, it is fleeting
Poetry, music, beauty
Tethered by gravity.
The trillium, their stems
And petals outstretched,
Dance in waltzes,
Exquisite trinities,
Graceful feet upon
A whirling planet.

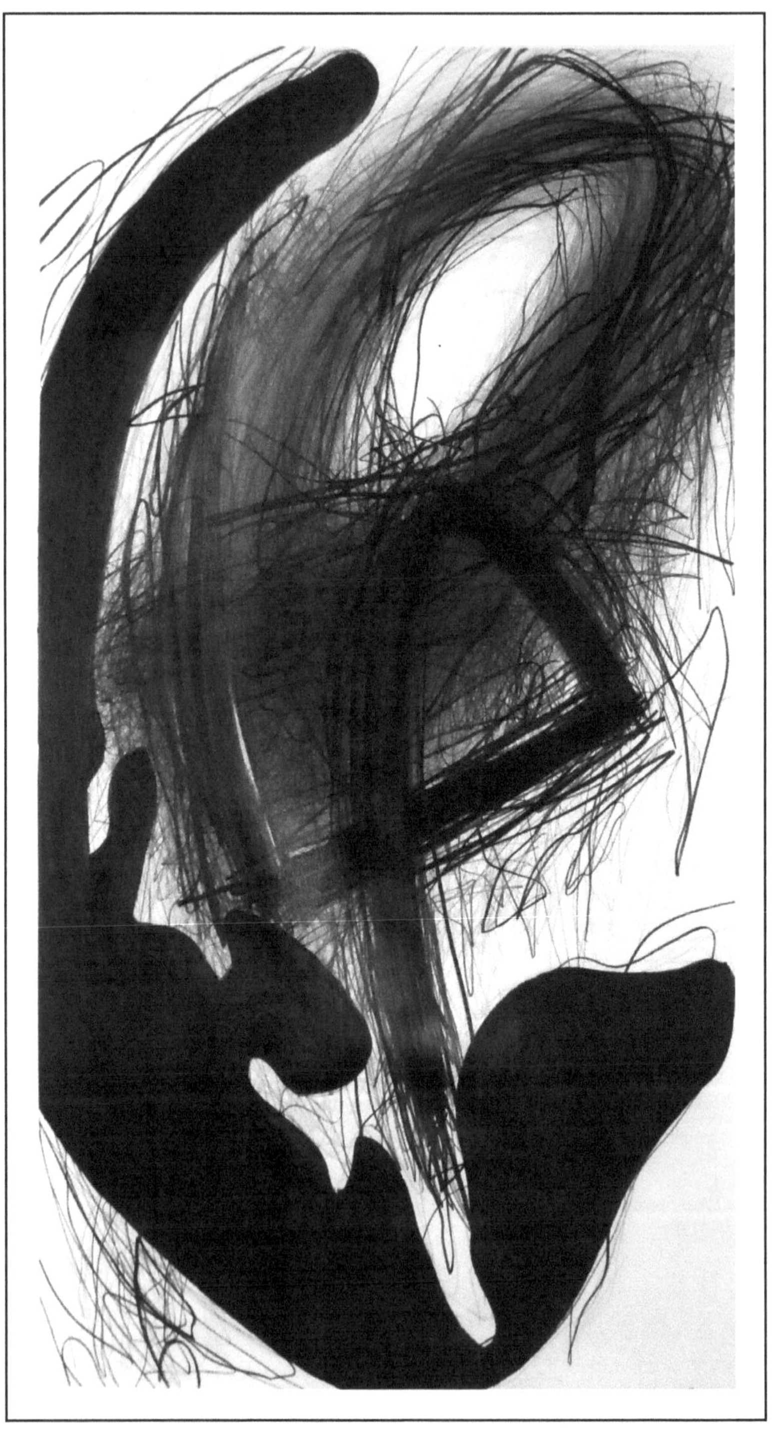

Certainly No Nirvana

Absolutely insane,
Completely unhinged,
Sign your commitment papers,
Bring on the straitjacket,
Thorazine, group therapy,
Long, contemplative walks
Round the asylum grounds.
To rid ourselves of suffering,
At-last-and-once-and-for-all,
Is your delusional plan.
Good God, man!
Without suffering, without
The chaos of greed and obsession,
Will you grasp the implications,
Imagine the pervasive tedium?
There'll be no thrill of karma,
Sin, our heady entertainment.
Everywhere there'll be
Contentment, a giddy laughter;
Stock markets will crash;
The snow leopard might survive;
Ten thousand species might thrive.
No Buddha, no Jesus,
Everywhere unemployed,
Panhandling popes, priests,
Monks, gurus, kings, cops,
All dogma a futile pursuit,
Certainly, no nirvana.
Madness, fool. Snap out of it!

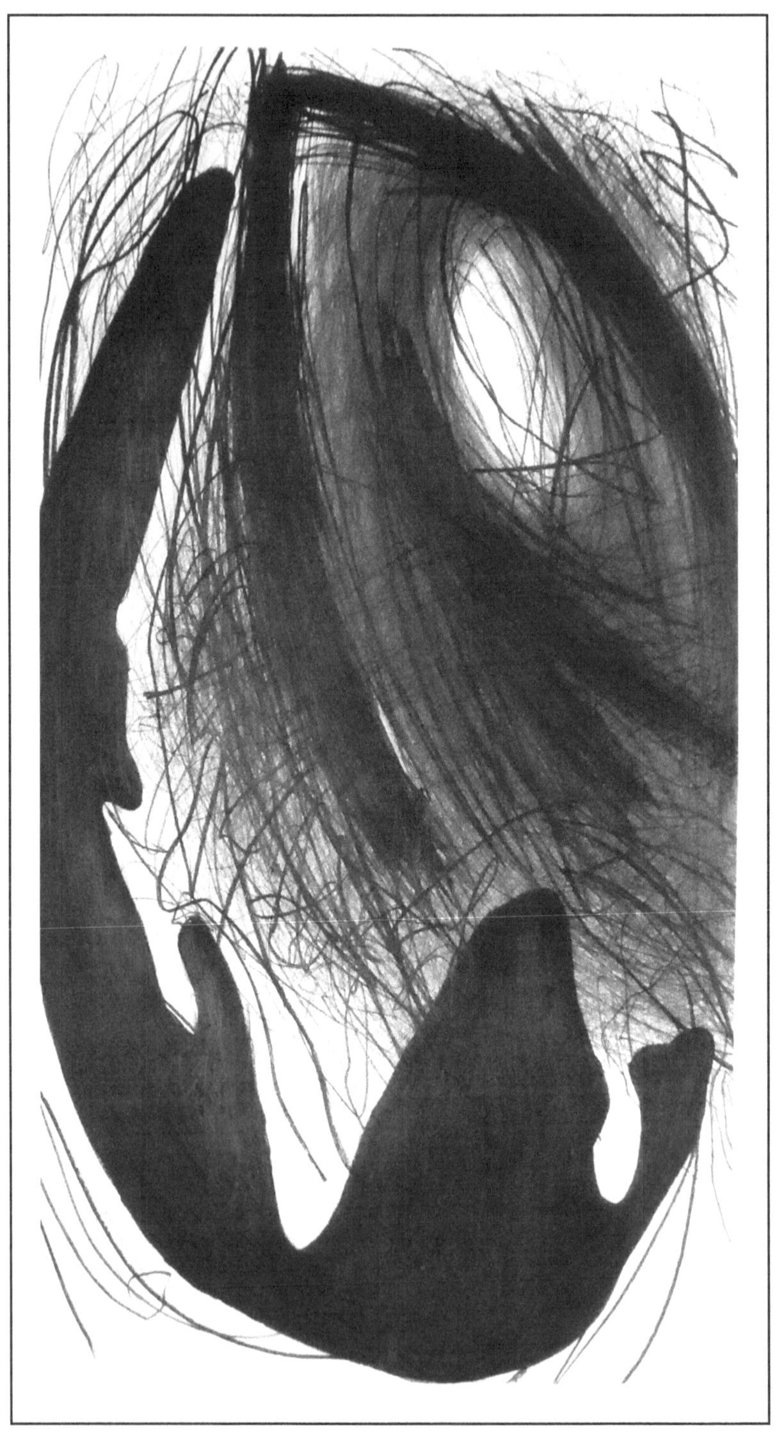

A Keening

Now a keening, piercing at every turn,
How did I arrive at this anguish?
My cry, now a predictable, animal shriek,
A poacher's snare in the forest, seeping
Into every pore, a pungent, exotic oil,
My mouth a chasm, teeth gaping,
Gulping at insufficient air,
My shoulders rattling, knees buckling
Of their own accord, my wail
Is not so tangible as for a death
(You lost your sister to heroin.
You lost your son to prison.
You lost your breasts to cancer.)
But a loss nonetheless, merely
A pervasive apprehension, a paralysis,
Run-away obsession, so staggering
Is the absurd, the random, irrational
Decrees, disparaging bureaucracy.
Where is the solace, a little levity—
In my monkish cell, my hermit's retreat?
I've been apprised, this dread is now
Routine and to be expected.

Despite Too Many

Despite too many tubes
Stuck in us
All that air and blood
Wending in and out of us
Us stuck upon a needle
(Please! We plead!)
And so many too many
There there theres
And pretty little pink
Pill after pill
Endearments
Dropped into us
Despite too many wires
Hooked up to us
Measuring calculating
Precise statistics
Despite all the beeps
Blips tics sighs
Our pals machines
(Who turned on the TV?)
Despite a dearth of hue
Everywhere white and white
Telltale tang of antiseptic
Despite all the plastic
Gloves masks walls
Deadly molecules splitting us
There is there must be
Love between us

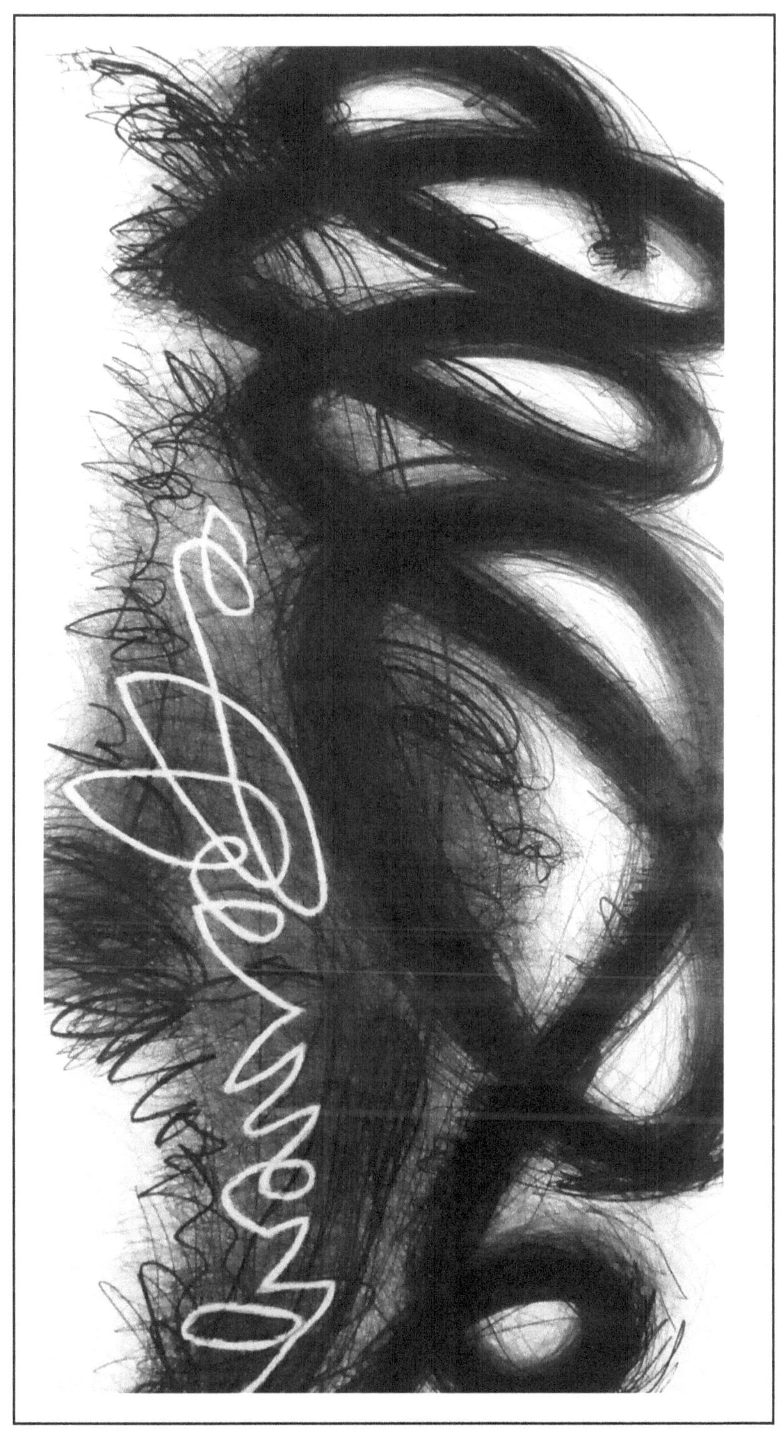

Hoarder

When I'm dead, a loony hoarder, what shall I do with this reservoir of *maya,* all this knowledge of the world? I've stumbled along with the illusion that this erudition is stored like so much grain in a silo (each kernel a . . . oh, never mind). Yes, I suppose amassing information was essential for my overall amelioration and a liberation from an ordinary outcome. But I am an old man; I've stockpiled plenty of facts. And I'm wondering if it is so very necessary to impress you with trivia in correspondence or conversation for a quiz show or a board game—to win, win, win. Which Prelude or Etude, which opus, which pianist? I know the music is Chopin and it is beautiful. This is enough.

Fra Filippo Lippi, an artist of the Quattrocento, professed his vows to the Church in 1421 and fell in love with a young nun, Lucrezia Buti. Lucrezia, her sister Spinetta, and five other novitiates lived in the monk's house. There were children and debts. Filippo was tortured on the rack. He seemed more preoccupied with love and painting than God or money. Cosimo de Medici pressed Pope Pius to intervene. What I know best—the fact is—tears came unexpectedly. While on a trip to Florence, I wept over his *Madonna and Child* in the Uffizi as I was missing my wife and son that day. (And there was something else, sublime and inexplicable, that defied measurement or aesthetic category.)

How may I accumulate this moment—this bliss? It is autumn and the leaves of this particular sapling (I am unacquainted with the phylum, genus or species, though I can muster *deciduous.*) are a vibrant yellow-green, a hue paradoxically more electric and subtle in the sunlight than chartreuse. Still clinging to the twigs, these hover, a composition above crimson and saffron. But my words are nothing. Come walk the woods with me. See for yourself. Together we'll be Hotei, astonished, laughing, and oblivious to any other noise or nonsense.

I harbor a notion in my eccentric head that in the end, it is all oodles of ephemera and weigh whether I've used this edification in pursuit of a good, quiet and simple life. This is a modest nirvana: finally never giving a damn about the details and dismissing all inadequacy over my lack of omniscience.

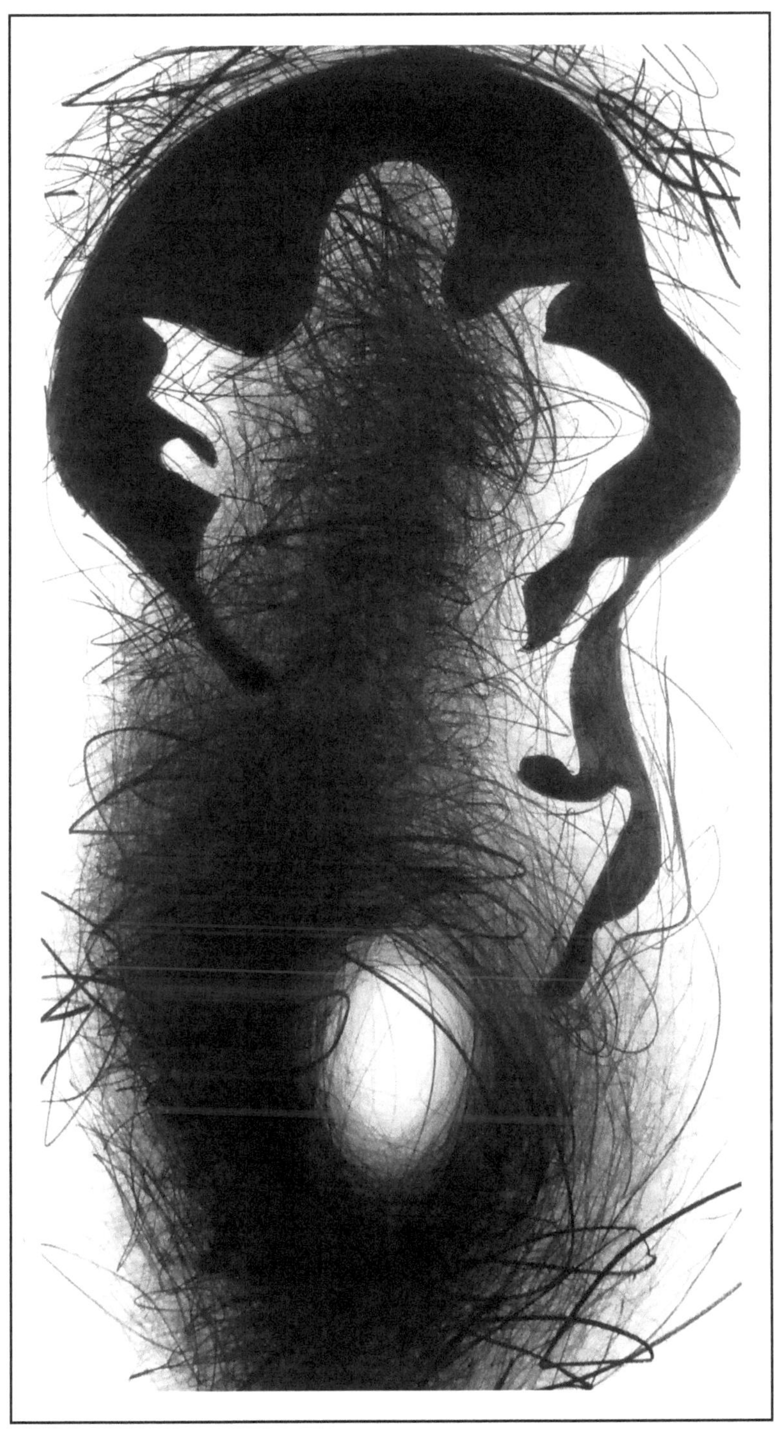

Intoxication

My flaw, our human situation, hopeless Adamite, I'm addicted
to suffering, stoned on karma, obsession my intoxication, a deluge
of thought a chaos, the futility of dramas rehearsed again and again.

My madness: my mind lacks a spigot to twist as I like. The meds,
the booze, the fix might slow the noise a bit, but drip, drip, drip,
eventually, illusion ebbs, veracity, rushes in, mania flows again.

Still, I learned, obsession reified in action is folly, problems and
beguiling solutions multiply, as prolific as stars. Though I pine
for a maelstrom of silence, only death brings solace. (Well, maybe,
maybe not. Usually, I'm not so pessimistic.)

In my utopia, I'll dam my misery, then pipe it all to any other
place, dear, dear neurosis. However, without suffering, there'd be
no Noah, no need for Buddha, Jesus, Allah, Rehab, no cathedral,
temple, mosque, all empty, too boring, the Word of God irrelevant,
love as uncontrived as rain.

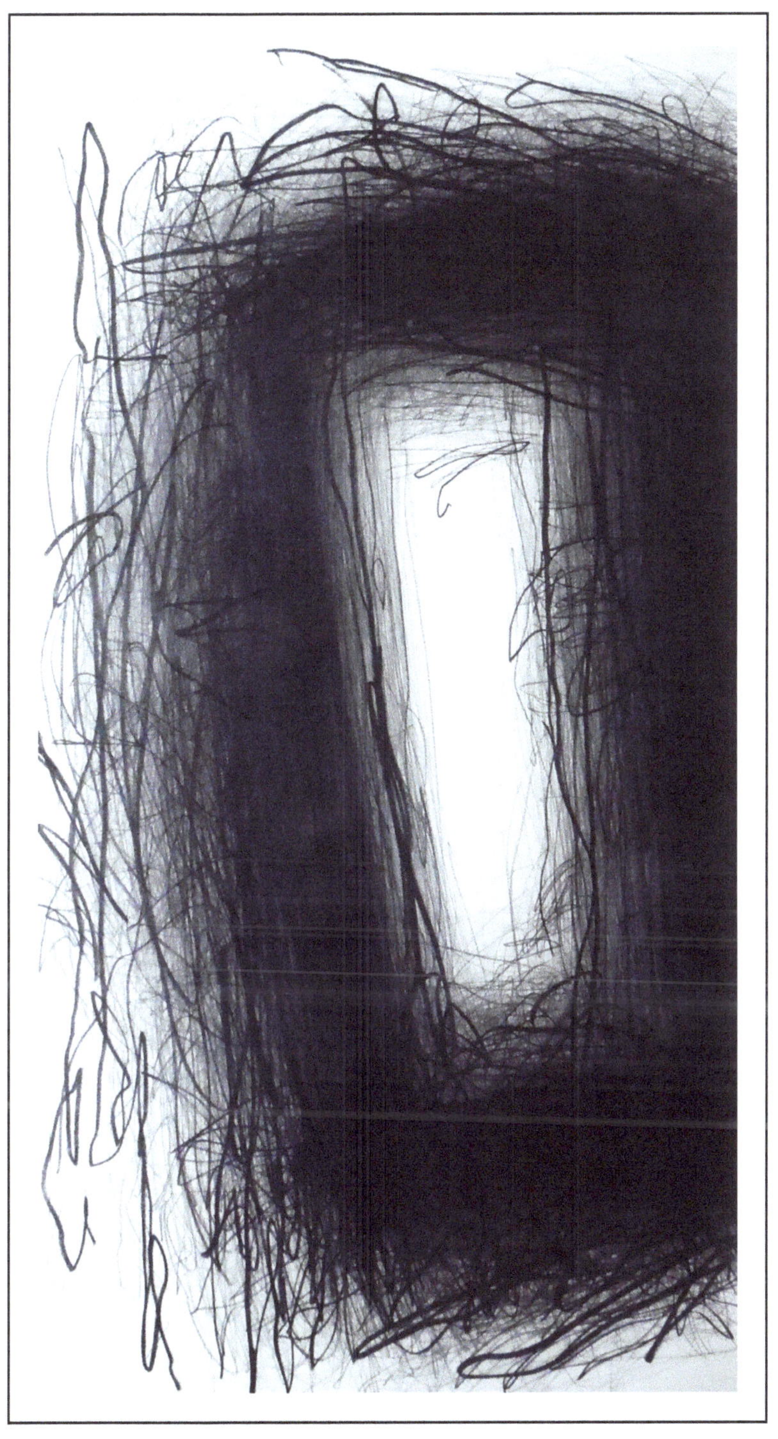

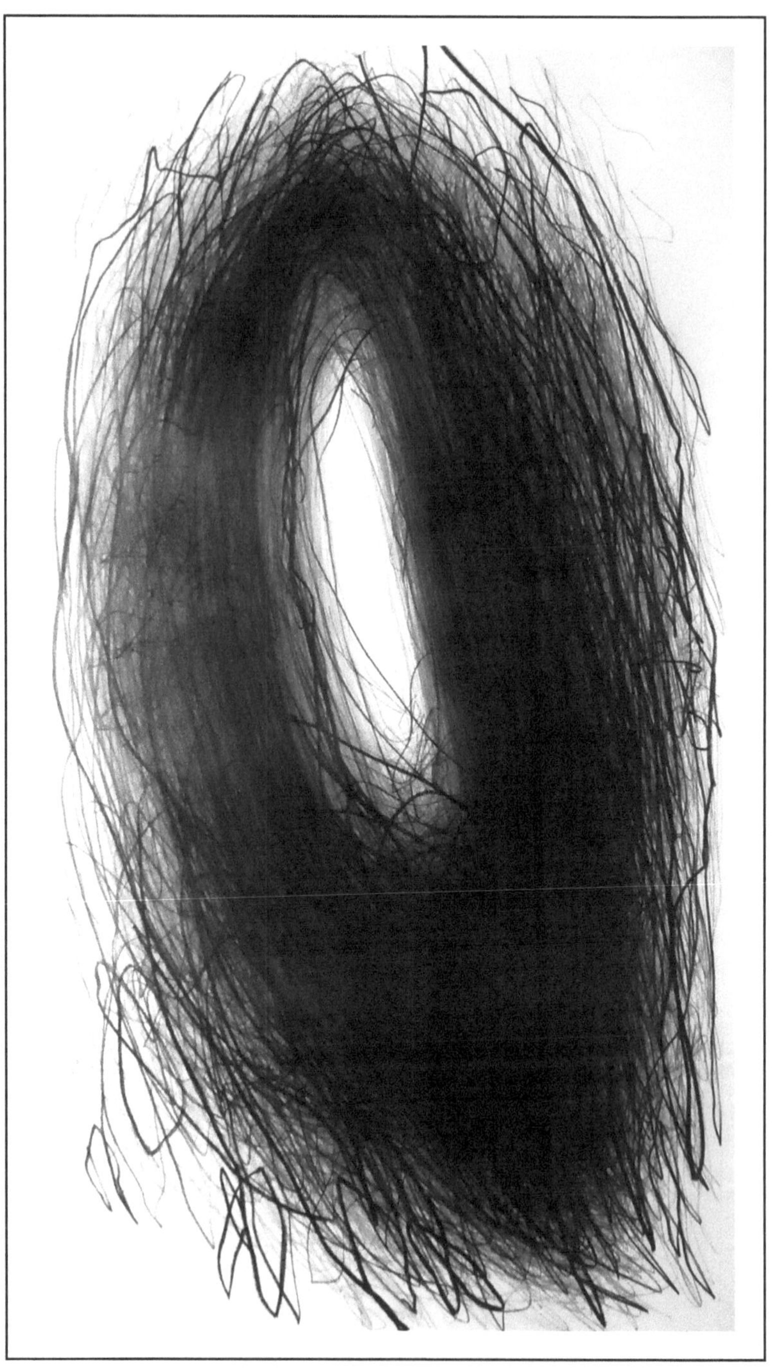

Nothing Left Undone

On this listless day
Of cold rain, *doloroso,*
Too gray, too gray, the hue,
A mourning dove's belly,
I'd rather it snow. Give me the
Beauty of a blizzard in January.
The trees wave, sway, oscillate.
Fine, the limbs do what they do
To merlot and a Chopin Etude.
And on impulse, I pick up
Lao Tzu—ridiculous, really,
But perversely comforting.
Round and round with him,
His absurdity, I'll go.
Speaking of unintentional
Immortality, I laugh out loud:
"One does less and less until
One does nothing at all and
When one does nothing at all,
There is nothing left undone."
Well then, I suppose I shall be
Lazy, at least for now, until
Motivated, until I pine for and then,
Of course, ruin whatever's
Bright and shiny and new.

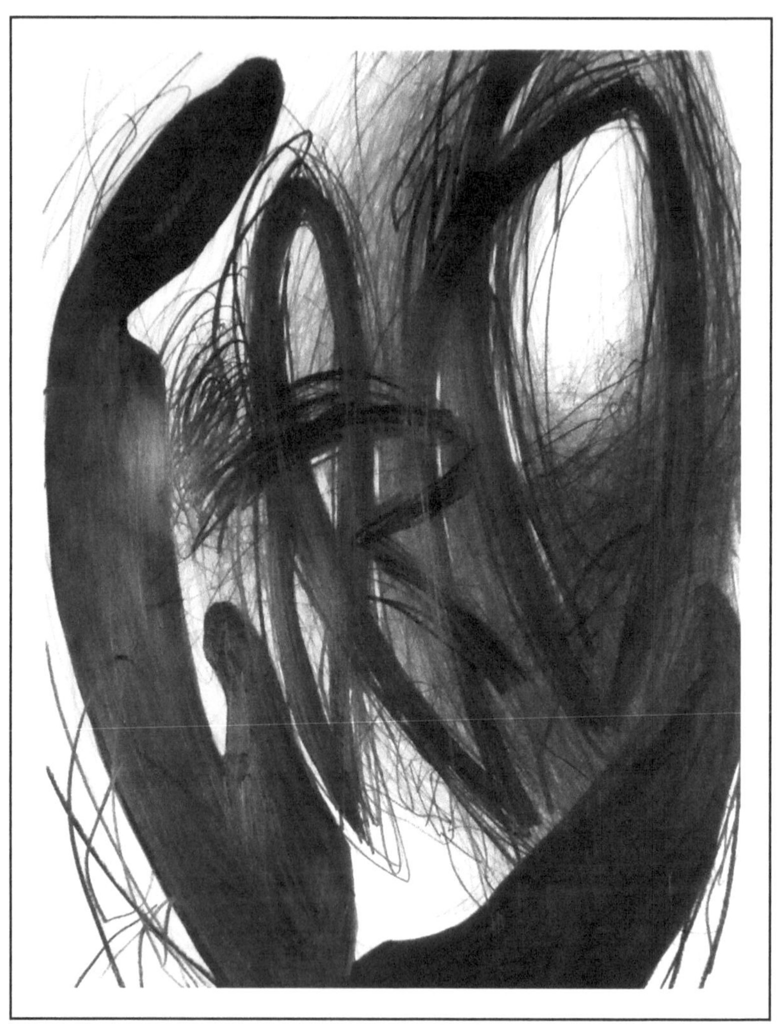

Seven Years

Seven years might do it, seven years of silence, seven years
at my age, an uncharted significance. I abandoned all
stratagem after seven years of battle, no longer inspired
to vanquish the absurd. The seduction garish, insistent,
an addict to futile solutions, I sought to quell the churning
chaos of human nature, to restrain our elegant destruction,
the relentless death of permanence—idealism, my childhood
chum, finally estranged. My regret: comprehension
arrived too slowly.

I shall endeavor (or endure) seven years of silence, though
an unlikely buddha, bumbling through karma, unversed
in nirvana. I shall likely fail. Will this silence be equally
clamorous, another predictable fixation, this shut mouth
simply another rickety construct? Will my lips be lazy fools
or screwed tight, a hatch holding back a muddy deluge?
My regret: compassion so vital, arrived too slowly. I wonder
if there will be a quiet life after seven years of silence.

Blissful Obliteration

This morning, fog obscures the sharp
Definition of objects, landscape, expressions,
Wings and foliage. I relish this as lately
I endeavor to become invisible or at least
Negligible, indistinct. I choose this
Blissful obliteration. If successful I'll
Vanish into mist, far beyond the Madonna,
The soft, dull, blue-gray cliffs of Leonardo's
Vinci in the distance. You, an acquaintance,
Or you, my best buddy, here near me are
Left with my silence. Discomfited, flummoxed,
You think me rude. Listen, you had your
Chance to hear me as a brash young man.
However, I harbor no grudge. I assure you
I am very much alive, maybe happy now
As my evaporation is nothing special, a mere
Plethora of quiet days. So far there is less
Suffering than in my previous aim for attention,
My hollow validation. Now I am a shadow,
Flimsy at the edges, obscured by the fog.

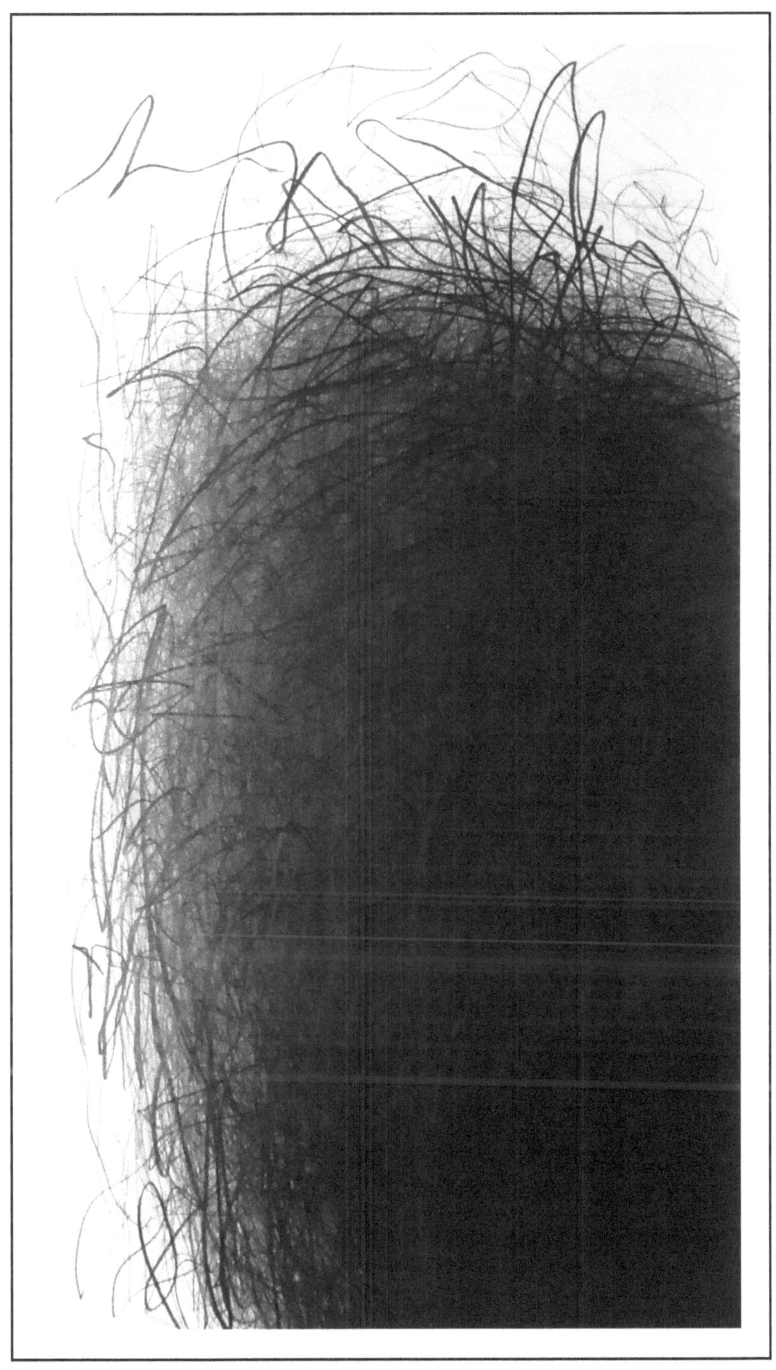

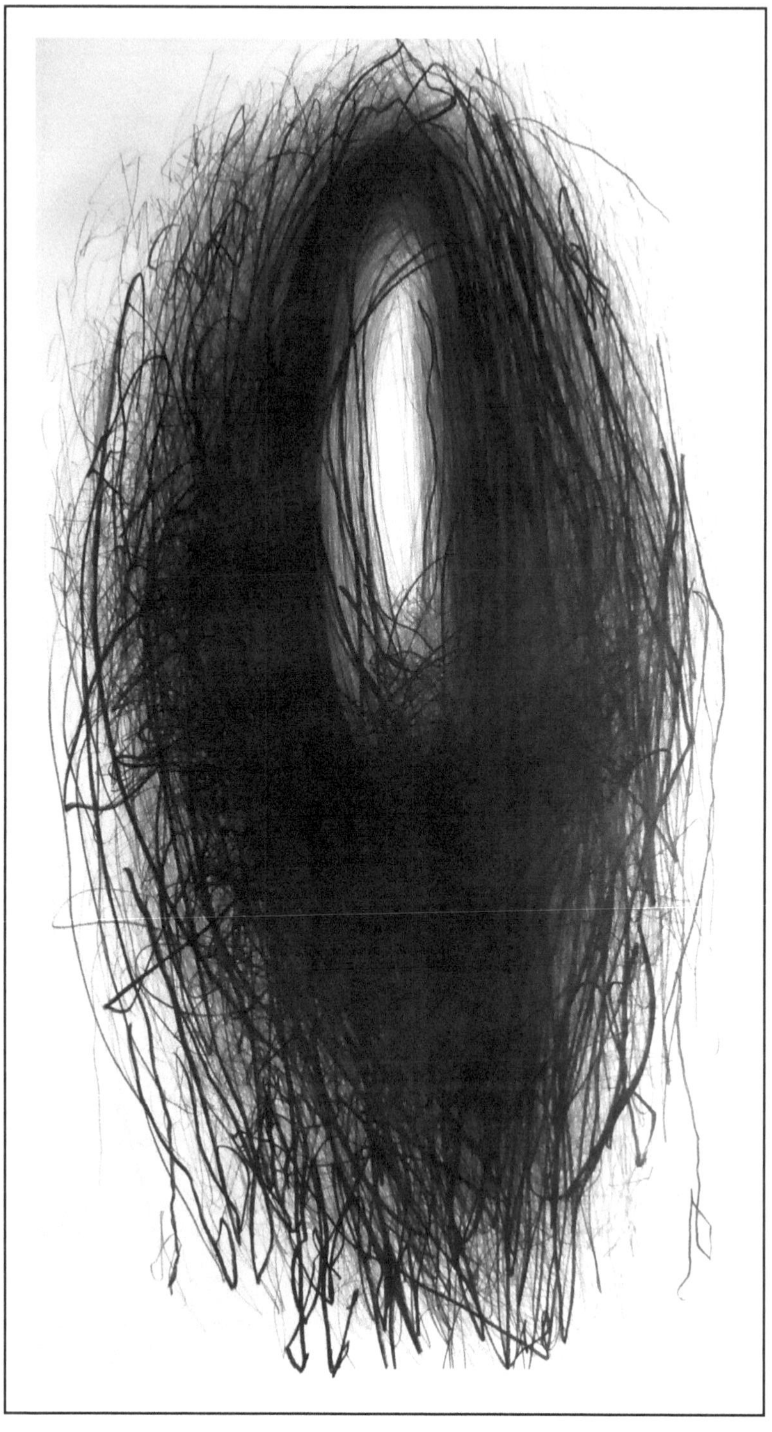

Love

Nirvana is a silly
Pursuit so long as there's
A semblance of hope
Of love, of love, of love.

It is in our nature
(Instinct or policy)
To cling to love,
To cling to the thrill, though
Love's brevity is suffering,

An expectation of illusion,
A small, fleeting comfort,
An elusive constant in
Our chaos, our violence.

We pine, we obsess,
We facilitate negotiations,
Then sanction the torment.
Tell me, tell me!
There is no alternative
To love, to love, to love.

Nirvana at Last

Nirvana at last,
Enlightenment for all,
A Second Coming came and went,
War, famine, religion all tidy,
Suffering allayed, sins absolved.
Pick your version of bliss:
Beulah or Elysium. S'all good.
At last, that's that.
Finally, prayer wheels needn't spin;
Rosary beads lose sequence;
The sun and moon skip a day
Without notice. Hold on!
So weary, waves cease their
Incessant lapping at the shore;
Trillium surmise, two petals, certainly
Two leaves, are preferable to three;
The leopard, now the narcissist,
Disinterested in stalking gazelle,
Is too vain, too fixated on his spots;
Swallows find their wings,
Such silly appendages,
To be superfluous.

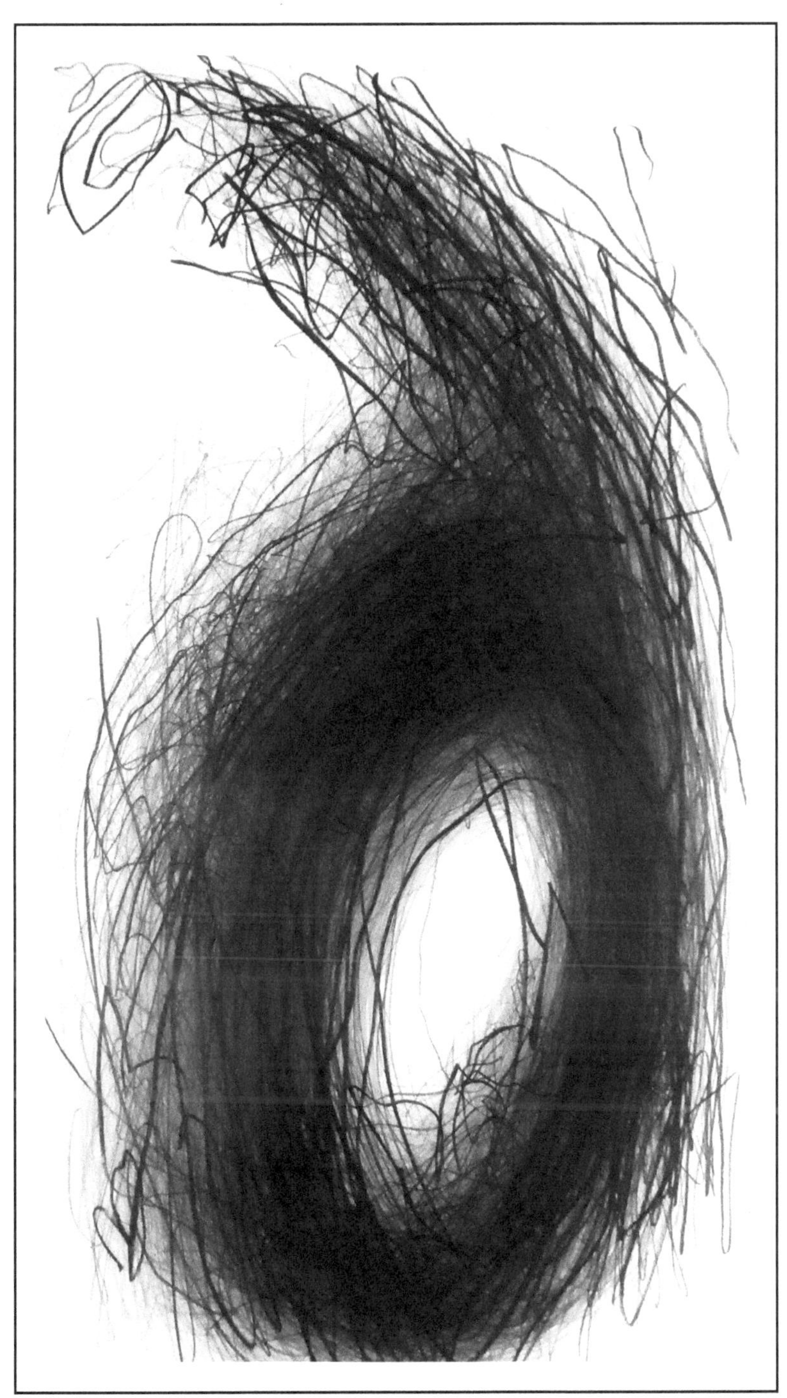

Practical

Like you, I open
My eyes each morning,
Astonished I'm alive,

Oh so exceedingly aware of
My clumsy mantra,
No, I'll be frank, simply,

An obsessive repetition:
"Quiet mind."
"Quiet life."

I demand, I insist,
And so, until I am
Dead, dead, dead,

This desire remains elusive.
(You must acknowledge the
Absurd, the anxiety, the rage.)

Anyway, in all this
Chaos, this is all
Wishful thinking.

I am weary:
Try, try as I might
To play the sage—

So futile, so silly—
Laughter is likely
More practical.

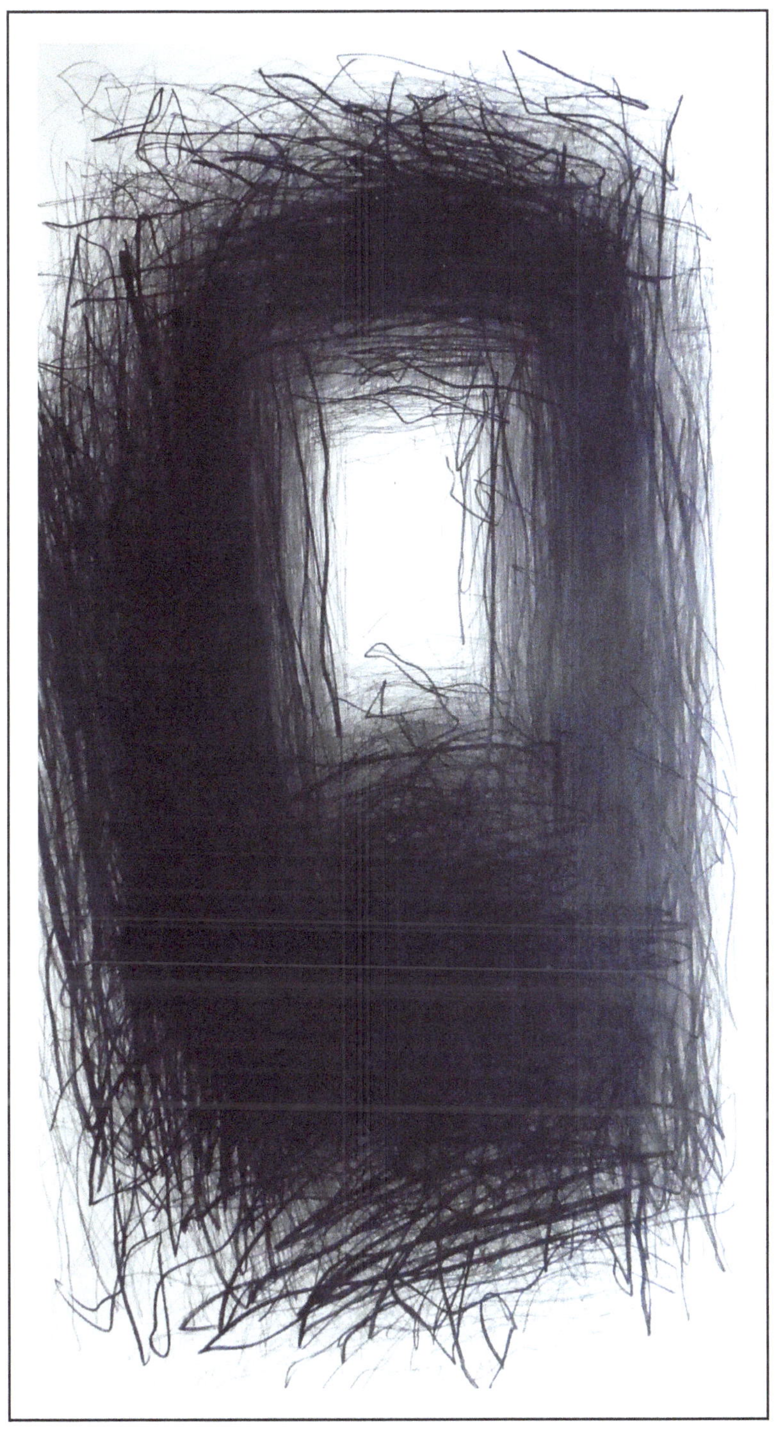

Little Boy

In my head I am
Yet a little boy
(At last at last!)
Shy impressionable fidgety
Frantic my mind grasps
For what's fleeting
My incongruity
With reality what's
Obvious is startling:
Damnable *duhkha*
My paunch my girth
My broken teeth
My plaintive joints
Sad saggy ass
Lethargy of reflex
Liverspotted hands
Tired old leopard
My accumulation
Of useless wisdom
Know this! (I say
Wagging a finger)
It's rare but there's
Such a state as
Naivete at sixty

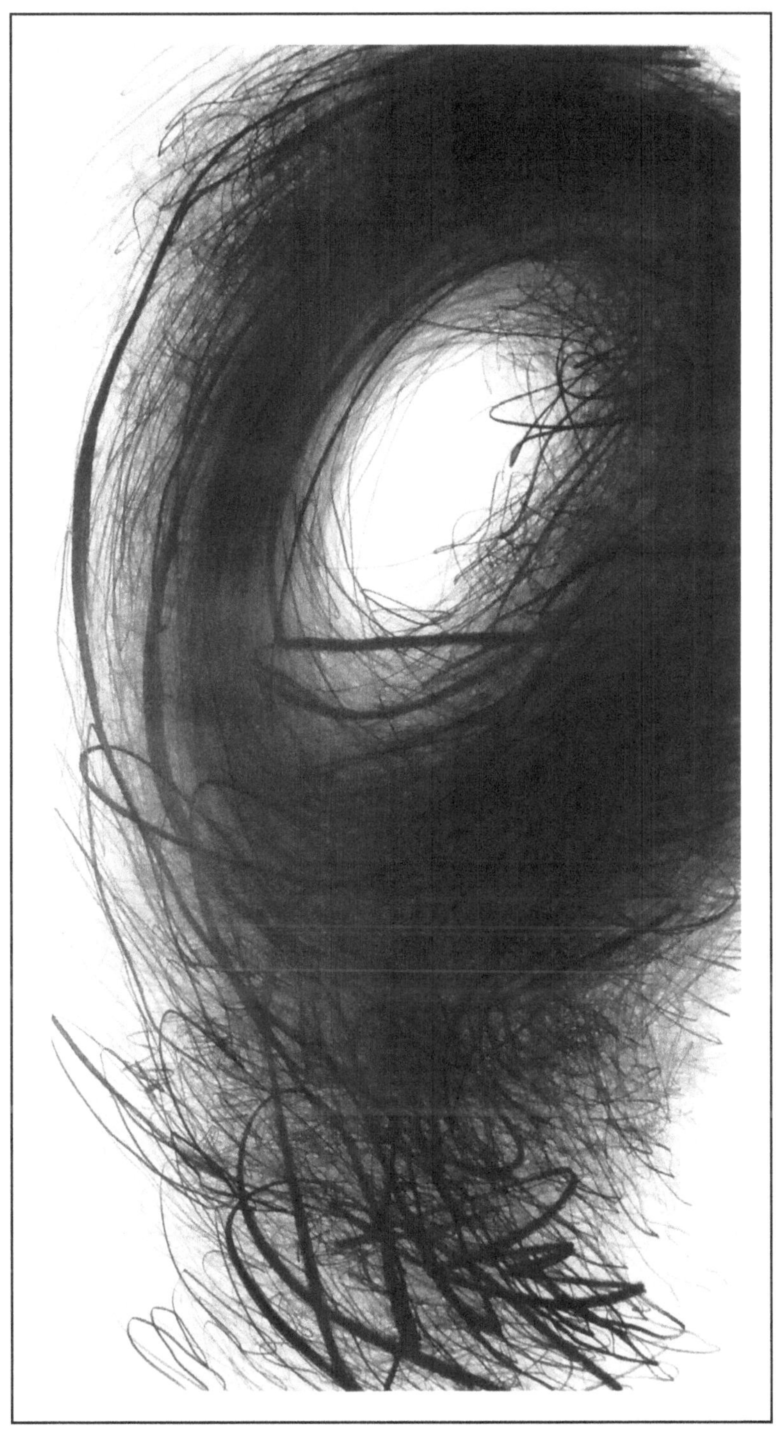

David Sapp, artist, writer and professor, is a native of the evocative landscape, vibrant light, gently rolling hills, and wide, meandering Kokosing River valley of central Ohio. He is a Pushcart nominee and the recipient of Ohio Arts Council Individual Excellence Award Grants for both visual art and poetry. His poems have appeared widely in many print and online venues across the United States, Canada, and the United Kingdom. His publications also include articles in the *Journal of Creative Behavior,* chapbooks *Close to Home* and *Two Buddha,* and his novel *Flying Over Erie.* His graphite drawings have been exhibited in solo, group, and juried exhibitions across the nation. He earned baccalaureate degrees in art and psychology and a master of fine arts in drawing. He teaches studio art and art history at a small Ohio college and lives with his wife, Heidi, along the southern shore of Lake Erie.

Allen Zimmerman was born and brought up in Thailand and was educated at an international school in South India, Oberlin College, and Columbia University. He received training in Chinese Mandarin at the Army Language School and was stationed in Taiwan. While pursuing graduate studies at Columbia University, he conducted research in Chinese poetry at Kyoto University on a Fulbright grant. He has taught at Connecticut College, Case Western Reserve University, the Osaka College of Art, and the Cleveland Institute of Art, where he also served as teaching Dean of Students. Courses under his instruction have included Classical Chinese Language, Chinese Literature in Translation, Ways of Thought: East and West, Brushworks: Creativity and Taoism, Classical Chinese Poetry, and Traditional Japanese Literature. He is retired as professor emeritus from the Cleveland Institute of Art. He and his wife, Edythe, now divide their time between Cleveland and County Kerry, Ireland.

www.ingramcontent.com/pod-product-compliance
Lightning Source LLC
LaVergne TN
LVHW052307100826
845147LV00006B/692
* 9 7 8 1 9 5 1 6 5 1 7 7 0 *